CUP OF *Chai*

WITH A THOUSAND INTERRUPTIONS

PARUL PATEL

BlueRose ONE .com
Stories Matter
NewDelhi • London

BLUEROSE PUBLISHERS
India | U.K.

BlueRose ONE
Stories Matter
New Delhi • London

For permissions requests or inquiries regarding this publication, please contact:

BLUEROSE PUBLISHERS
www.BlueRoseONE.com
info@bluerosepublishers.com
+91 8882 898 898
+4407342408967

ISBN: 978-93-7310-114-9

Typesetting: Sagar

First Edition: December 2025

To my daughters, thank you for bringing the beautiful mess that makes life worth writing about.

The beginning

As I wait for the school bus to arrive, a small daydream takes over, a vision of the kids heading off, their voices fading as I wave goodbye. Soon after, my husband leaves for work, and the house finally exhales, wrapped in a still and quiet sigh that stirs a flicker of excitement in my stomach.

Sipping my tea, my mind drifts back to when we were newlyweds. I remember how he used to notice the smallest details, letting me choose the TV show or take me out for my favourite ice cream. Those tiny gestures, so full of care, once defined the language of love for me.

Now, standing by the window, I watch the motionless trees, their branches unmoving in the crisp air. I can't help but wonder where it has all gone. The innocence of my children, the warmth of my husband, the compassion that kept me alive.

Who am I, what is my purpose and my identity? Am I just a mother or a wife or a daughter?

29th Jan 2025

The alarm blared at 6:30 a.m., and I dragged myself out of bed to wake my elder daughter, Aliza, only to hear her announce that she couldn't go to school because her leg hurt from football practice. A familiar sense of dread washed over me, and if you've ever been in my shoes, you'll know exactly why. I had been plotting, very deliberately, to shoo all my family members out of the house so I could breathe in peace, but luck has never really been on my side.

I called the doctor and managed to book an appointment, carefully double-checking the time with my daughter. Somehow, though, my husband still managed to make me the villain of the situation, criticising my wildly unrealistic expectation that our daughter could wake up, get dressed, and eat breakfast, all within thirty minutes. By that point, I was fuming. Still, I kept it to myself, swallowed my pride, and pushed through the day.

Once I was back home, I tried to settle at the dining table, my usual spot for writing. Just as I was beginning to find my rhythm, my daughter interrupted me. And then again. And then again. By the tenth interruption, she was asking for something so trivial that I cringed with embarrassment on her behalf.

What is it with teenagers? Do they all lose their brains somewhere along the way and then collect them again once the phase is over? Clearly, it wasn't just my patience wearing thin. I must have had plenty of it, after all, if she felt comfortable enough to ask me something silly for the tenth time without hesitation.

By then, I had started fantasising about the day ending, about finally collapsing onto my bed, blissfully alone, with no noise, and no questions.

Reflection of the day:

I can't tell if I crave solitude or if being alone would only leave me hollow. Maybe I just miss adult conversations, when you can speak freely about anything and still feel like yourself. It's a bit ironic, isn't it?

30th Jan 2025

After yesterday, my younger daughter Rumi decided it was her turn to take a day off because she firmly believes it is her birth right to have everything her sister gets to have.

So, she dropped a bombshell on us this morning. She announced that her head, yes, her head, had been hurting because of some fall at school, which I was really hoping was imaginary.

I called the paediatrician in a hurry, and Jeh, my husband, decided to come along with us. It was stressful, but I quietly enjoyed the fact that I was getting some time with him to chat and just catch up on the way to the doctor's clinic.

We had so much to talk about, especially with a few short trips coming up that we hadn't had the chance to plan. Sitting in the doctor's waiting room for an hour actually gave us the rare opportunity to chat without interruptions. Rumi, who's just eight, was completely oblivious to our conversation, happily scribbling away on her LCD tablet. This wouldn't have been possible with our 13-year-old in comparison. She's 13 going on 30 who acts like a proper little detective, spying on every word when we're discussing something remotely fun or indulging in a bit of harmless gossip. The only time she tunes us out is when we mention homework, chores or cleaning.

After returning back, we settled for a non-welcoming lunch, leftovers from last night, since our cook is on leave for a few days. (I'll share more about my cooking adventures in a later chapter. It's really not so bad! I've even figured out how to whip up fancy meals with just a bit of prep work from my staff. I'll share my tips soon, so stay tuned.)

The happiness was short-lived. Jeh hesitantly decided to take Rumi to her gymnastics class to inform her coach to be careful with her head for a few days. In the rush, she forgot to take her water bottle, and suddenly, my husband, my lord and master, started blaming me for not having it ready in time.

Why, I ask, should I be responsible for organising the water bottle when he, as the parent taking her to class, could have easily handled it himself? I understand that it doesn't naturally occur to him that kids need water bottles every time they step out, but does that mean I'm automatically expected to provide this service? Who granted him the right to demand this from me? Why couldn't he figure it out, put two and two together, and just do it?

While this ruckus unfolded, Aliza started asking me to switch on the Wi-Fi booster because she couldn't connect to her online class. Again, why couldn't she get up and handle it herself? At that moment, I couldn't help but feel like a butler, silently fulfilling everyone's demands while swallowing my frustration and keeping my mouth shut.

Reflection for the day:

A little time spent with your spouse can truly lighten your mood. It's amazing how just being heard and having a moment together can lift your spirits. I'm feeling really happy, and I'm hoping we can do this more often. However, I will prefer this without any head injuries involved!

31st Jan 2025

What a day! Supervising our new office construction made me feel like I have an actual role beyond being "just a housewife." Honestly, thank goodness my husband keeps throwing these small projects my way. I feel valuable, even if it's not about earning money. It's more about lending an extra hand, which gives me the rare pride of calling myself a working woman. That said, I have absolutely no idea how to define my job description.

I mean, what am I exactly? A manager to my family? A PR representative? Event planner? Holiday planner? Household CEO (yes, I have staff, but someone has to run the show)? Occasionally, I moonlight as my husband's office and factory "odd-job" assistant. Oh, and let's not forget my roles as the emotional gatekeeper, fitness coach, and unofficial family nutritionist. There really should be a title for all of this, but sadly there isn't.

On a brighter note, my cousin-sister-in-law dropped by for a quick coffee before jetting off on her travels. These little human connections really do wonders for the soul. They remind me that while family is important, friendships and bonds outside your home are equally vital for staying sane.

I even managed to call my mom today. It was going well until she started reminding me how little I visit Delhi with the kids. Apparently, I'm failing as a daughter because I haven't packed up my circus to fly off every few months. I don't think she understands that the kids have school, and I have a life here. It's not exactly easy to just drop everything. Honestly, being in a different city from them sucks. If they lived nearby, I could leave the kids with their *Nana-Nani* and sneak off on holidays with my husband guilt-free. What a dream.

Reflection of the day:

I'm happy being a mom and a wife, but I'm still searching for something that truly fulfils me. Non-family, non-household projects give me a kick and for now, that's enough to keep me going.

1st Feb 2025

I told you I could cook!!! But the reason I was cooking is less exciting. My cook hasn't been coming because of certain health issues, and it's that dreaded time of the year when the other house help disappears for their annual back-to-home trips (hello, December, January, and February blues). It's a Saturday, the kids are home, and I recently treated myself to an Instant Pot.

Now I know the Instant Pot is old news for people abroad, but for me, an Indian living in India, it still feels like a small miracle. I got it as an anniversary present for us, but it's become my new best friend. Buying it gave me the same thrill I felt at my first late-night party. I know, I know, call me aunty or oldie, but this is where my life is at right now.

Back to the Instant Pot. I think my mom would be proud of me. She's not just a great cook, she's Michelin star-level (3 stars, thank you very much). And today, I made *chana dal vegetable pulao* all by myself! Well, okay, my kitchen help did all the chopping and prepping, but hey, I was the one who bravely pressed buttons and threw everything into that shiny pot. Later, with my chest puffed up in pride, I told my friends about this victory.

But the genuine payoff came quietly, later in the day. My kids ate it without complaining, without scoffing, and without pushing the food around on their plates. I had actually put food on the table, cooked with my own hands (and my awesome new Instant Pot).

Oh, and let's not forget the almond flour chocolate chip cookies I baked. Gluten-free, baking soda-free, made with jaggery instead of sugar, basically, a health freak's dream. And guess what? They turned out so good that my kids devoured them and asked for more. I felt like a supermom.

Growing up, I avoided the kitchen like the plague. I'd always seen my mom there, pouring her talent into every dish, but she never got credit beyond the title of "just a housewife." And now? Now I've realised cooking isn't some trivial chore, it's an essential life skill and a survival tool. Actually, it's a superpower.

Reflection of the day:

It's easy to underestimate a housewife, until you realise her hands keep the wheels of family and life turning, one ordinary meal at a time.

2nd Feb 2025

Sundays are everything to me, well I still love my kids but Sundays are my days. No alarms screaming, no frantic, "Where are your socks?!" or "The bus is about to leave!" drama. Today felt even more special because Rumi decided to crawl into bed for a cuddle. For once, I wasn't in my usual role as the family's wake-up call operator. We snuggled for a while, and then she dropped the sweetest little "Mumma, I love you." Just like that, my day was made.

There are two things in life that can energise a mother instantly. Its either a full night's sleep (which is mythical), or some unexpected love from your child.

I decided to spoil my family with all the love and food they deserved.

And so began my kitchen marathon. Breakfast kicked off with a hearty egg casserole. Next, I moved on to mutton curry for lunch, which felt very satisfying because the Instant Pot makes me feel like I've put in way more effort than I actually have. That thing deserves an Oscar for best supporting Kitchen Appliance.

But my cooking didn't stop there because Aliza walked in with a request that made me question her sanity. I stared at her like she had just asked me to build the Eiffel Tower with biscuit crumbs but then she gave me the look. She asked me to bake 50 almond flour choco-chip cookies as her friends were coming over. And just like that I found myself "Blink-it-ing" all the ingredients. Watching the kids polish off these cookies was rewarding, but it left me contemplating one of life's greatest injustices. How do they stay so carefree, while I just inhale the smell of melted butter and gain a kilo?

Dinner was mac and cheese with veggies, a comfort food with a slightly healthy twist, because I convinced myself that throwing in a few greens balanced out all the cheese. By 3 pm, I had officially conquered the kitchen and fed everyone like a pro and honestly, it felt great.

Of course, Sundays don't let you off that easily. Jeh and I had to squeeze in a visit to the construction site for some office planning because, as it turns out, the to-do list doesn't take weekends off either.

But, the cherry on top of this busy day was picking up my cousin from the airport. She's my *maasi's* daughter, and growing up, we were as close as it gets. She's the closest to my age among all our other cousins, and we happen to share a huge collection of stories together. She told me she's bringing old childhood pictures, and I couldn't wait to see them. There's something so special about revisiting those carefree days when life was simple and the biggest fight we had was over who got the larger share of Maggi.

I was also secretly hoping she'll remind me of something about myself that I've completely forgotten, like a hint towards a tiny puzzle piece of who I used to be. I want to share those stories with my kids, too, so they can see a side of me beyond "the mom who nags about homework and messy rooms."

Reflection of the Day:

Why am I so obsessed with looking back at my childhood? Maybe it's because that's the truest version of myself. Maybe those childhood pictures and stories are little breadcrumbs leading me back to who I was and reminding me that she's still in there somewhere.

3rd Feb 2025

I hadn't felt this anxious since my first board exam. The fear was setting in, knowing that I would be managing the household with almost no staff. My cousin is visiting, and I found myself in the awkward position of having her prepare her own breakfast and lunch. But before you label me the worst host ever, know that cooking for 40 people is a breeze for her. So, I promise, I'm not that clueless or selfish.

After our kitchen escapades, we decided to treat ourselves to a salon visit. A hair wash where someone else does all the work, followed by a quick pedicure, has an odd way of tampering with your self-perception. You feel like such a goddess that you start believing you could walk the ramp for Paris Fashion Week.

We got home around the same time as the kids returned from school. One child was sent off to a class, while my cousin and I took the other to her gymnastics session, a class she had enthusiastically approved. Yet, enroute, we faced three meltdowns, when she declared her newfound passion for tennis.

"Mumma, you never do anything for me. Why can't you hire a tennis coach for me?"

So now it's my fault for not recruiting a top-tier coach to train her.

For what exactly, Wimbledon?

Over coffee at a nearby Starbucks, my cousin, who doesn't have kids, remarked that enduring labour pain might be easier than navigating these daily dramas. I couldn't help but agree. Later, we took a leisurely walk at the local club, chatting about everything and nothing. We reflected on how our lives had turned out, the things we're grateful for, and the things we regret. It was nice, actually, because it forced us to pause and really reflect on ourselves.

Dinner was a quiet affair; we were all so drained that the silence was a welcome respite. I lacked the energy for the usual dinner table aggression and "I hate you mom" glances!

Once the children were asleep, we stayed up late, chatting until the wee hours, just like old times.

Reflections of the Day:

Whoever said labour pain is intense has clearly never tried raising children.

4th Feb 2025

Hello sore throat!!! As if God hadn't tested me enough, now I had such a delightful challenge to face! Body ache was the main course with headache as the side chutney.

Over the years, I've become best friends with my local chemist. I call him at the drop of a hat, describe my symptoms, and he kindly obliges by guiding me and prescribing the necessary medicines. "*Bhabhiji*," he'd say, "*I think you must take this medicine; it will sort you out in two days, and you'll be back on your feet.*"

The universe knew I needed a quick fix, so I called my dear drug dealer (aka my local chemist *bhaiya ji*). My husband has always made fun of me for consulting a local chemist instead of a professional doctor. Anyway, who has the time to go to a doctor when your local chemist *bhaiya* has become your family, nurturing you like your own mother would? Mind you, I'm away from my whole family; not even a distant cousin lives in my town. So,

I've had to build my support system from scratch, and the local chemist is definitely at the top of my list.

Of course, I sometimes also call a few friends who have doctors in their family to consult them on my behalf and get back to me with a complete diagnosis of my issues.

Here I was, knocking back one *adrak chai* after another as if I was having shots, getting through the day, and saying goodbye to my cousin, hugging her, and promising to visit her in the US.

Reflection of the day:

Take care of yourself, because no one else will. Your family believes you're invincible. It's quite cute, isn't it? They think I'm God.

5th Feb 2025

Today was supposed to be my day off after a hectic few days! You know, one day where I won't jump like a ninja at every task thrown my way. But my husband has gotten so used to seeing me whip out my phone and take notes like a secretary every time he starts listing things that he didn't even pause to check my mood.

When I didn't immediately start noting down his list of points on my phone, he looked genuinely puzzled. Usually, I'm in full manager mode, setting reminders, and even offering to send him reminders for his errands because, "poor guy, he works so hard all day."

Meanwhile, I'm just a humble housewife, a title many seem to think comes with a luxury package of lounging on the couch, sipping fancy coffee, and getting foot massages. Sadly, none of those perks are included. Do I wish that were my reality? Absolutely. But the reality of being a stay-at-home mom is far from the luxury-filled fantasy people imagine. Quite the opposite, really.

I gave up my clothing line when I was eight months pregnant with Aliza. I like to do one important thing at a time because it is not in my nature to dabble. I had to choose, and I picked the obvious. When I love something, it becomes my entire identity. So, I shut shop and devoted myself fully to motherhood. And I mothered well. But somewhere along the way, I mixed up my purpose in life with motherhood itself. I lost myself in the process.

Then came Rumi.

At eight years old, she already has opinions about the colour and fit of my dresses. She loves drawing, usually women dressed in different styles. She wants to be a fashion designer and keeps asking me to restart my business so she can "design with me." I pray she keeps that fire alive and stays unstoppable in whatever she chooses. I hope she remembers she is allowed to be many things, even when life tries to pull her in only one direction.

Do I regret having children? Absolutely not. My girls are the favourite part of my life. They are my pride and joy. But they are not the entire story of who I am. And yes, I know I might be judged for saying that. I still don't feel any guilt.

I feel like something else is waiting for me. I just don't know what it looks like yet. Maybe I will return to fashion. Maybe I will build something completely different. Or maybe there is nothing for now, and I am alright with that too.

I do not need to be remembered by everyone.

I just want to be remembered by myself again.

Speaking of squabbles, the "highlight" of my day came during a showdown with my daughter. I confiscated her phone because of mountains of unfinished homework, and she retaliated in front of my in-laws by declaring, "Mom doesn't do anything these days except obsess over her Instant Pot. She's just bored all day!" Ouch.

I played it cool, though, and quipped, "Exactly! That's why I need your phone to entertain myself." But inside? Yeah, that one stung. And the irony? The same Instant Pot, she had accused me of obsessing over, is what makes their dinner appear out of thin air every night!

It's wild, isn't it? The constant need to justify your existence just because you're a stay-at-home mom. And the worst part is, it's not the men. It's our own. Women measuring women. Who is achieving more, contributing more, living a life that seems more respectable to the outside world. We put each other down not because we're cruel, but because we've all grown up being told that our worth has to be earned. That it must be visible to count. So instead of standing together, we compare. We confuse our fears for facts. When, in reality, we should be uplifting one another.

And, hey, if all I really do is sip coffee and twiddle my thumbs, someone please direct me to the spa where my imaginary foot massage is waiting.

Anyway, Jeh took my side in front of everyone like a true hero. But later, in private, he casually asked, "*When was the last time you talked nicely to the kids instead of just asking them if they've finished their homework or chores?*" And just like that, I was questioning my parenting skills.

Here's the thing, whenever I try to talk nicely, I get no response! Zilch. So then, of course, I have to raise my voice to get anything done. And let me tell you, the mother-daughter dynamic is a whole different ball game compared to the father-daughter one. He gets the sweet hugs and giggles; I get the homework and screen time fights and tantrums.

And don't even get me started on the guilt trip about me not wanting to hang out with the kids after 9 p.m. Apparently, I'm the only mom in the entire world who demands some me-time after bedtime. Like I'm some kind of alien! But, if I took a global poll right now, I'm pretty sure I'd win by a landslide. Moms everywhere would agree 9 p.m. is officially "off-duty" time.

Reflection of the day:

No matter how hard you try to explain yourself, you will still be misunderstood! So, save your energy and spend it on something worth your while. Maybe like a foot massage!

6th Feb 2025

We went to our farmhouse site today for my husband's dream project. He loves nature, while I'm all about brick and mortar. He can lose himself in the trees, come out all zenned, and probably compose a poem. But, if I lose myself in the trees, they'll haunt me in my nightmares forever.

But hey, it's his dream, and I'm kind of the one executing it. Though to be fair, he's put his heart and soul into that land planting trees, fruits, and veggies, carefully deciding their placement for perfect views from the house. Very poetic. Meanwhile, I'm busy focusing on the biggest fish in the pond: the interiors and aesthetics. Because, the furniture better match the curtains if I'm expected to spend time there.

On the way home, we got into a deeply thrilling conversation about plumbing. Yes, bathroom plumbing. I suggested he get the repairs done while I visit my parents this summer since it'll take a week. His response? *"Oh no, you won't be there to supervise!"* I mean, he's a grown man, but apparently managing minor plumbing without me is like solving a Rubik's cube blindfolded.

Anyway, back home, I was greeted by my next delightful project: packing for Aliza's school trip to Goa. She's gone ahead and added 395,830 items to the H&M cart, complete with a PowerPoint presentation on why she needs every single one of them for a 4-day trip. Thinking back, I was probably the same at her age. Girls and the "we-can-never-have-enough-clothes" syndrome, it's a rite of passage.

But now, it's my turn to play the villain. I have to rationalise, and somehow convince her why 40 outfits aren't necessary. I was pretty sure this task would cost me a decade of my life, so I poured myself a super-strong cup of coffee, the only joy I'd have in the next 9,345 hours of sorting, negotiating, and compromising. Yay. I was so excited. (Not.)

Reflection of the Day:

At some point, your child will be a mirror of yourself, leaving you stunned for a moment, then laughing because, well, karma's a genius.

7th Feb 2025

Went to the tile shop today to pick tiles for the new office. Because, of course, that's what housewives do, pick tiles. Isn't it just the most housewife thing ever? Anyway, I walked in knowing exactly what I wanted: classy, matte tiles which are understated. But the tile guy had other plans who decided his life's mission was to sell me these shiny, fake-marble disasters.

"*Madam, these glossy ones will make your office look so fancy*," he said, chewing on *pan masala* and almost spitting it out mid-sentence as he spoke. I smiled politely, but in my head, I was already imagining myself slipping on those slick tiles and breaking my already injured back. I tried hinting that I wasn't interested, but this man was relentless. Why do people assume "no" is just an opening bid? So, in the end, I had to be assertive and make my decision clear. Now I'm probably labelled as the rude lady in his book, but honestly, I'd rather be called rude than spend every day staring at those shiny tiles and regretting my decision.

Back home, Rumi came to me with her demand of the day: she'll only go to gymnastics if I get her new sports outfits. Because, of course, how well you can stretch depends entirely on how fashionable you look. This kid, I tell you.

The evening was a breath of fresh air, though. Jeh and I actually made it to a party. Dressing up after so long felt incredible. I forgot all about dinner for the kids, but no worries, McDonald's came through with Happy Meals, which made everyone perfectly happy.

The weekend's lined up with social events, and for once, I'm actually excited. Let's see how long this optimism lasts.

Reflection of the Day:

Sometimes, being "rude" is just being firm in your choices. And if that makes me rude, so be it.

8th Feb 2025

The Goa trip shopping saga continued today, and this time it was just me and Aliza at the mall. We wandered into Nykaa, which I knew was a big mistake from the time we walked into the store. Why do cosmetic stores always smell like so much perfume? I'm convinced their business model is to knock you unconscious so you buy things in a daze. How else would they sell that glittery purple eyeliner? While Aliza was in her element, tossing face packs into her basket like she was stocking up for the apocalypse, I could feel a migraine creeping in.

Then came a makeup list from Aliza. She told me very considerately that I could veto two items from the list, and she'd only get the rest. "How fair," I thought. Until it occurred to me. This little mastermind had strategically added two items she didn't even want, knowing very well I'd veto those and unknowingly let her walk away with everything she actually wanted. Thirteen-year-olds are too clever for their own good sometimes.

Of course, I couldn't say no outright. Oh no. Because if I did, I'd be that mom, the one who refuses to buy makeup for her 13-year-old when every other mom is out there gifting their daughters entire Huda Beauty collections and hiring makeup artists for their birthdays. At thirteen, I wasn't even allowed to think about makeup, let alone wear it. My mom didn't believe in negotiations, or arguments. It was ONLY her way. End of story. Times have certainly changed.

After surviving the shopping ordeal, we came home. Since it was a second Saturday and school was off, Rumi had gone to the factory with Jeh, leaving just me and Aliza for lunch. It was actually lovely, just the two of us sitting together, chatting over food. Moments like these don't happen often, and I was savouring it... until my migraine decided to ruin the party. I ended up in bed, praying for my head to stop throbbing. When I finally woke up, Jeh and Rumi were back, and thankfully, I felt human again which was perfect because Saturday night plans were calling.

Jeh and I got dressed up and headed out for a play and dinner with friends. It was exactly what I needed. For a few hours, I forgot about migraines, makeup lists, and the terrifying realization that my 13-year-old might actually be smarter than me.

Reflection of the Day:

If you think you're outsmarting your child, think again. They're just letting you believe that while quietly staying two steps ahead of you.

9th Feb 2025

Today was one of those Sundays that can only be described as... uneventful. Where nothing groundbreaking happens, and the highlight is that you managed to step out for a game of bowling and dinner with friends. But we'll get to that part later.

The day started as it usually does with me chasing after the kids to finish their homework and trying to tackle the numerous points on my to-do list. Sundays are my "wrap up loose ends" day because half the things on that list need Jeh's input, and Sunday is the only day he's home long enough to give me his undivided attention. (Well, undivided-ish, but I take what I get.) However, today something snapped in me. Or maybe it un-snapped. I just threw my hands up in surrender and said, "Not today!" No homework nagging, no to-do list ticking. Instead, I had lunch, crawled into bed, and treated myself to the most blissful nap of my life.

That sleep was something else. It was as if my body finally exhaled after holding itself together for far too long. I don't know if it was inspired by the reels I've been bingeing on Instagram lately, but there was this one book someone recommended about how you can "see things clearly only when you slow down." Naturally, I ordered it immediately on Amazon, because obviously I don't just want it, I need it, and Jeh would back me up on this. But since Amazon takes two days to deliver enlightenment, I decided to just embrace the title and slow down for the day. If I hadn't, I would've never discovered the sorcery of an afternoon nap, it was so deep and relaxing that it practically reset my entire personality.

When I woke up, I was a new person. Sweet. Calm. A loving mom and wife, not pestering anyone about anything. My family was... confused. They've always said I'm perpetually wired, running on some secret mission that no one else knows about. So, to see me so chill was both delightful and mildly alarming. I could see it on their faces, this mix of "Wow, this is nice" and "Wait, is she okay? Does she still care about us?" It's fun to mess with your family like that sometimes. Keeps them on their toes. After all, a little existential panic about whether Mom still loves you isn't the worst thing. Maybe they'll value me more now.

Anyway, after this unexpected transformation, we headed out for bowling with friends. I was feeling confident, ready to conquer not just the bowling alley but maybe even a neighbouring country. But here's the thing about bowling: confidence doesn't matter if you don't have hand-eye coordination. After a series of embarrassingly bad throws and thoroughly letting my team down, we all decided to blame the bowling lane. Something had to be wrong with it, it couldn't possibly be our lack of skill.

Post-bowling, we went to a *dhaba* for dinner. It's that enchanting time of year when you can still sit outside and enjoy the weather without sweating buckets. Continuing with the bowling theme, someone suggested we go around and share what "bowled us over" about our partners. When it was my turn, I proudly announced that in my case, it was love at first sight. Before I even spoke to Jeh, I knew he was the one. It was hilarious hearing everyone's stories, so sweet and entertaining. By the end of the night, we were laughing so hard that my sides hurt.

Reflection of the Day:

Never underestimate the power of a good nap. It might just make you a better person!

10th Feb 2025

Weekends are tricky. On the surface, they seem fun, but for women, they bring their own set of guilt trips. After three nights of eating out, I woke up feeling like I had personally betrayed every salad leaf I've ever eaten. Now, Jeh? Oh, he ate his naan and butter chicken without a care in the world. But for us women, there's this unspoken rule that we should feel bad for enjoying food. I mean, why are we conditioned to believe that one extra bite equals failure? Society has set such ridiculous expectations on women to look a certain way, and we buy into it like it's on sale.

Of course, I made the usual resolution, my 100th, if anyone's counting, that I was done with outside food and would start eating healthy. I took it so seriously that I worked out like my life depended on it. By afternoon, I was so drained I could've fainted. But here's the thing: as a woman, you don't get to faint. You've got a house to run, kids to look after, and the daily madness to handle.

Take my kids, for example. They're adorable, but they have the eating habits of royalty. Both want completely different snacks, so I ended up making two. Because why not? Who needs rest anyway? Then, there was the architect at the office who needed me for some electric work discussion which I don't understand a thing about.

By the time the kids got home, I was on my last legs. First, I had to convince them to eat the snacks I made. You can't just demand these things anymore. Oh no. In this century, moms have to negotiate with their kids.

Then came gymnastics class for the younger one, while the older one needed to be chauffeured to another class. I felt like a person who'd been awake too long, very irritable. But hey, Jeh had promised to cook dinner, and for once, I thought I could sit back.

Turns out, his yoga class got delayed, and he decided that meant dinner was my responsibility again. I was this close to losing it, but instead, I did what women always do, I just got on with it. Exhausted but determined, I managed to put food on the table.

At dinner, I told Jeh he was in charge of the kids and had to make sure they finished their dinner, took a shower, and got ready for bed. Then, I went to my room, ready to unwind in front of the TV.

Five minutes later, guess who showed up? Jeh.

"*Did the kids eat? Are they in bed?*" I asked, already suspicious. He gave me a casual, "*Yeah, yeah, all good.*" But of course, all was not good. A little investigation revealed that the kids were still at the table, only halfway through dinner and nowhere close to bed. So, guess who ended up dealing with everything? No prizes for the right answer.

Reflection of the day:

Society expects women to do it all, but next time, I'm expecting Jeh to actually do what he says.

11th Feb 2025

I just couldn't bring myself for my morning Pilates routine today. Whether it was the soreness from yesterday's workout or sheer lack of motivation, I'll never know, but it just wasn't happening. Instead, I found a creative solution, a.k.a. guilt-driven productivity. Thanks to my current staffing crisis, I decided to jump in and "help out" by doing *jhadu-poccha*.

Now, this wasn't some charitable act born out of pure selflessness, it was me convincing myself that scrubbing floors could replace a workout. And it did! Strength training? Check. Cardio? Double check. I literally couldn't feel my legs halfway through the floor.

I haven't touched a broom since the lockdown days of 2020 when we all suddenly had to double up as domestic labour. Back then, I was younger, fitter, and clearly delusional because today, I felt every single squat. This little episode brought me a newfound appreciation for my house staff. The smile on her face when I said, "*let me help*," was priceless probably because she knew I'd regret it the moment I started.

Speaking of regrets, as I huffed and puffed through those 40 minutes, I realised this was easily the equivalent of two Pilates classes, minus the bullying voice of a trainer telling me to "engage my core." It made me think of the automation spree I went on during Covid, buying a dishwasher, a dryer, and even a Chinese version of a Roomba that only works when it feels like it. But after today's high-intensity workout, I decided to finally silence my stingy side and order a Dyson. Why should anyone, especially my staff, have to toil away like it's 1950 when technology exists to save us all? I still remember the wonder in my staff's eyes the first time she loaded the dishwasher. She called it a "magic box." I'm now determined to bring more magic into her life.

Later in the afternoon, Rumi returned home and asked me if she could style me in a tone dripping with sweetness that parents know is a trap. Now, I'm all for her budding love of fashion, but I was already eyeing the couch for my well-earned afternoon slump. But then came the "pleeeeaase" with her million-dollar smile. I stood no chance. And just like that, my lazy afternoon plans vanished, replaced by me becoming a mannequin. Was I stylish? Questionable. Did it make Rumi happy? Absolutely.

In the evening, it was Aliza's turn to keep me on my toes. It was her monthly braces checkup, which, as fate would have it, is in the same building as Starbucks. No sooner had we left the dentist than she requested me for a Starbucks Mocha Frappe. Here we were, fresh out of a lecture on oral hygiene, and she was begging for a sugar-laden, caffeine-spiked dessert!

As her mother and unofficial health guardian, I turned her down with all my might. I swear, that place is the root of all parenting woes. It wasn't Aliza, but Starbucks that was the problem! Why does it exist in every corner of the world, waiting to test my willpower? Naturally, my refusal gave my daughter the permission to say sweet things like "*You're so controlling*" and "*I hate you!*"

I love my life.

Reflection of the Day:

Forget the guilt and order a Venti Frappe for myself next time.

12th Feb 2025

My day kicked off with pure rage. The fabricator, in all his infinite wisdom, decided to install the window grills in front of the windows instead of behind them. So now, after all our hard work to make the farm feel like a serene nature retreat, it looks like Central Jail. Who even does this? And this is after I've told this man at least a thousand times to inform me before taking any action. But, does his thick skull absorb anything? Of course not. Because it's already packed to the brim with male chauvinism.

Okay, I know I've ranted before about how women are conditioned to be more sacrificial, but this man is living proof of what's truly wrong with our society. He simply does not believe in listening to me. Not because I'm unclear. Not because I'm unreasonable. But, just because I happen to be a woman. Like, really? It's 2025.

Anyway, Jeh and I rushed to the farm site, for corrections, well, I rushed, Jeh conveniently tagged along. Any excuse to skip office and head to the farm, and he's like a bee to honey. But this time, he hijacked my trip, which was fine... except for one major problem. He refused to let me play my music in the car. I love music and it's a long ride.

At the farm, I took it upon myself to roast the fabricator in front of everyone. Not because I'm a terrible person, but because he absolutely deserved it. Even Jeh, the one who always tells me to "be polite" because he thinks I'm too blunt, gave me a thumbs up.

Jeh doesn't get it, though. Unless a woman is firm, people don't take her seriously. If I had politely requested, he move the grills, he would've probably welded them tighter.

While I was having the time of my life yelling at this guy, Jeh, on the other hand, was frolicking through the farm, plucking mulberries from trees he had planted himself. He was absolutely glowing with self-satisfaction. You'd think he had just discovered agriculture itself. The way he cradled that tiny handful of mulberries, you'd think they were Olympic gold medals for Farming Excellence. Meanwhile, I was still mentally plotting the fabricator's downfall.

Honestly, though, Jeh is a different person at the farm. While I'm busy dealing with contractors and making sure things don't go horribly wrong, he just wanders off, inspecting trees like a proud plant father. Checking their progress, asking the caretaker if they're getting enough water, probably whispering words of encouragement to them. I argue with men; he bonds with trees. That's our dynamic at the farm.

On the way back, we somehow got into a heated debate about exercise. I do Pilates; he does yoga. And today, he was on a mission to convince me that yoga is superior. According to him, I was wasting my time on Pilates, and I needed to see the light. I tried to explain basic human logic, that, just because something is "better" doesn't mean I will enjoy it, and if I won't enjoy it, I won't be consistent. And consistency trumps superiority any day.

But no. He wasn't hearing it.

Thankfully, before things escalated further, ABBA's "Slipping Through My Fingers" came on, and we both became an old uncle-aunty duo reminiscing about how our eldest had "grown up too fast." It was quite the mood shift.

Later that evening, my entire staff (both of them, and yes, I know I've complained before about my bare-minimum staff situation) had an event to attend. They had told me long ago, and I was actually a little excited, because this meant the kids would have to fend for themselves for once.

The four of us, me, Jeh, and our two kids, had to divide all the chores. Laying the table, heating the food, washing the dishes, loading the dishwasher, cleaning the kitchen... basically, doing the "invisible labour" they never think twice about. I was secretly thrilled because this was going to be an educational experience. And guess what? It totally worked.

They definitely gained some perspective. The realization was sinking in, that plates don't magically clean themselves, and the kitchen doesn't auto-reset after dinner. I swear, the impact was as strong as a Taylor Swift breakup song. Life-changing.

Reflection of the Day:

The next time my staff wants to take a day off, I will 100% let it happen... for educational purposes, of course.

13th Feb 2025

As Jeh was leaving for work, he noticed his shirt was tearing at the elbow. Not surprising, considering he practically lives in the same two shirts on rotation. And why? Because those are the only shirts he likes to wear. Sometimes I wonder if he is more loyal to Uniqlo or me. The problem is that this specific style has been discontinued both online and in stores.

But it doesn't stop him from hoping. Every so often, he makes me check online, convinced that by some miracle, Uniqlo will resurrect his beloved shirt just for him. And now, because the universe refuses to bend to his wardrobe wishes, he's asked me to find another brand that makes an identical shirt, same design, same fit, same fabric, same everything. Not "similar." Identical.

I didn't even bother arguing. I just nodded and said, "I'll check." We both knew I wouldn't. This was one of those "Yes, darling" moments where I pretend to care, let him believe I'm on the case, and then move on with my life. I mean, if Uniqlo themselves have given up on this shirt, why am I expected to fight fate?

Well, anyway, today was an exceptionally auspicious day, balance was finally restored in my universe. Why? Because all my staff, who had collectively decided to abandon me for their well-earned leaves, had come back. The house is no longer in survival mode, and to celebrate this monumental occasion, I did the only logical thing. I took off for a coffee date with a friend and a long, leisurely walk with another friend afterwards. Because now I just can!

Those carefree, college-days feeling of roaming around with no real purpose? That was me today. These days, kids are being raised by a carefully curated mix of parents and nannies, not the whole joint-family brigade like in the good old days. And today, my modern-day *parivaar* replacement, a.k.a. my staff had officially resumed their duties. So, while they handled the important things (keeping the kids alive), I did what any responsibility-free adult would do, I gallivanted around town, blissfully, soaking in the sweet taste of *vella giri*.

Reflection of the day:

While Jeh chases shirts that don't exist, I enjoyed the things that do which are coffee, long walks, and the joy of my staff being back. Balance restored.

14th Feb 2025

I had a frank discussion with my mother-in-law today.

Growing up, my mom always said, "*The kitchen is the root of all family fights.*" As a kid, I never really understood how a place that smelt like *ghee*-soaked *parathas* and *masala chai* could also be the site of such intense warfare. But here I am, years later, still trying to figure out why kitchens turn into war zones.

After a long discussion over how things should be done, we decided to amicably separate our kitchens.

I still don't know if it's because younger people just have different needs or if both sides feel misunderstood or if it's simply a battle of who gets more control. Maybe I'll understand her side when I'm older. Or maybe I'll just keep guessing forever. Until then, all I know is that I'm *not* old yet.

But it's funny how life comes full circle. As a child, I'd watch my mom in the kitchen, doing everything, being told how to do everything, and just going along with it. And I'd always wonder, *why is a full-grown woman in her 40s listening to someone else about how to cut onions?* It made no sense. I swore that when I grew up, I'd never do that. And yet, here I am, almost 40, pretending like I'm not adjusting when, in fact, that's exactly what I'm doing.

I remember questioning my mom about it. "*Why don't you just tell them off?*" And she'd shake her head and say, "*You won't understand now.*" I always thought that was just her way of dodging the question. But now I see, it wasn't about giving in, it was about keeping peace. About choosing battles. And compromising. And I suppose I'm doing the same now.

That being said, I also decided that the cycle stops with me. I have two daughters who are watching and learning. One day, they'll be in their own kitchens, dealing with their own dynamics. And if there's one thing I want them to take away from all this, it's that their mom didn't just adjust, she made choices. She set boundaries. Because it was another way of maintaining peace.

Anyway, moving on to something far more important, Aliza's Goa trip!

A school trip is basically an excuse for excessive snack shopping, so obviously, we went all in. As I watched her grab packets of chips and enough chocolate to start a small business, I had one of those *parent moments* where you wonder whether to say something responsible or just let it go. I went with the responsible route. I gave her a whole lecture about healthy balanced choices, and how "we don't need that much junk."

And then, mid-lecture, I had a flashback to my own school trip. To Goa, no less. I had stuffed my bag with an obscene amount of Crax and Hully Gully and had no regrets. And here I was, all these years later, playing the role of the concerned mother when, really, I had been just as bad, if not worse. Hypocrisy? Probably. But parenting is mostly just trying to guide your kids while conveniently forgetting your own not-so-wise decisions.

At the end of the day, I just hope that when I'm older, I understand my kids the way they need me to. And that they have the patience to understand me when I become the old, opinionated, snack-hoarding lady who still can't believe how expensive everything has gotten.

Reflection of the day:

Must steal some yummy chocolate for myself from Aliza's stash.

15th Feb 2025

Forget the sun, today, even the moon must have risen early, because my daughter, who considers 11 AM an ungodly hour, was up at 8 AM sharp. Not only up, but bouncing with the energy normally reserved for Ed Sheeran type concerts. Why? Because she was leaving the next day on her school trip.

Now, "excitement" would be an understatement. This child, who usually needs five wake-up calls and won't budge unless her mom's blood is boiling, was wide awake, knocking on our door, waking up the parents instead. She had not only woken up early, but had also packed. I mean, I know I'll still be up till 1 AM fixing it all, but in her mind, the macro packing was done. By 10 AM, she had chalked out her entire day like a CEO planning a product launch.

Jeh, ever the hands-on dad, had taken the day off, and together they had shopped for more snacks, stocked up on travel medicines, packed the camera and made a list of phone numbers to call during emergency. This was a record. Usually, the floor of her room looks like a crime scene where a tornado met an explosion, but today? I could see actual floor space. She had moved all her junk and put things in their right places, all so she could pack efficiently. If only school projects brought the same level of dedication.

And then, there was the hair struggle.

Now, apparently, it wasn't just a trip but a battle against humidity, a competition to see whose hair could stay anti-frizz the longest in Goa. So, Aliza and all her friends had collectively decided they wouldn't just get a blow-dry, but full-on hair straightening. Now, as a mother, I have two instinctive responses to things like this. Panic about hair damage and trying to find the least damaging way to give in anyway.

Determined to keep her hair looking great without destroying them, I took her to this spanking- new salon in town. Now, we live in a small town in India, so this salon was a big deal. They use only Dyson hair equipment, and if you've never heard of Dyson, just know that it's the Louis Vuitton of vacuum cleaners and hair gadgets. Basically, if something could straighten her hair without frying it, it was this.

So, there she was, getting the least-destructive, most luxurious hair straightening of her life, and there I was, feeling oddly proud of myself. Because this is what parents do. We happily spend money on our kids, getting them the best of everything, but when it comes to ourselves, we'll contemplate for a month before buying a new pair of socks.

Why do we parents do this? Why do we gladly swipe our cards for stuff like Legos, and once-in-a-lifetime experiences for our kids, but when it comes to buying something nice for ourselves, we hesitate like we're about to make a life-altering decision?

Reflection of the Day:

It's perfectly fine to treat yourself to a Dyson hair-dry once in a while. But first, survive the 1 AM packing marathon.

16th Feb 2025

It's 5:30 a.m. The day has arrived. It's Sunday, but there's no sign of a lazy morning because today is The Goa Trip.

Now, I have one question. Why has the school asked us to report three hours early? Are they secretly flying these kids to the Maldives instead of Goa? Do they need time to process their visas, clear immigration, and stamp their passports? I mean, seriously, it's Goa.

Standing outside the airport in 16 freaking degrees, waiting for every parent to arrive, was about as thrilling as watching paint dry. Jeh and I actually debated whether we should go this early, but Aliza was so hyped, she wanted to report five hours before departure because, in her head, an entire series of hurdles could stop her from reaching Goa. What if the car breaks down? What if we forget the way to the airport? What if time mysteriously moves faster today than on other days?

So, we negotiated her paranoia down to three hours, which felt like a fair compromise.

But honestly, it's not just the school's fault. We Indians have our own version of ETA. In the rest of the world, ETA means "Estimated Time of Arrival." In India, ETA stands for "Extra Time Allowed."

There are always those parents who only know this version.

Anyway, Aliza was so thrilled, her excitement made it all worth it. Watching her squeal and jump with her friends was so sweet. We waved her off and did what any rational parents would do after sacrificing sleep for this monumental event.

We went back home and passed out.

Now, here's the thing. Suddenly being responsible for one child instead of two felt like someone cut my workday from 12 hours to 6 hours. The sense of freedom was overwhelming.

And what do people do when they don't know what to do with themselves?

They start "organising their lives."

I decided to take on the single most exhausting task known to humankind: figuring out what everyone in the house should eat. Breakfast, lunch, dinner, snacks, for fifteen days, to be repeated for the next fifteen.

I strategised and calculated. I studied everyone's moods, cravings, and unreasonable demands. By the end of it, I had created something so brilliant I was convinced no one had ever dared attempt it before. Or at least, that's what I told myself to stay motivated.

Not only does the plan have a fixed menu, it also comes with recipes. Courtesy of my silent business partner, a.k.a Google. Now, instead of explaining to the cook for the millionth time how to make *aloo sabzi* without peas, I would simply hand over my creation, and just like that, my kitchen would practically run itself.

I might have just invented something genuinely life-altering and efficient. Honestly, I could sell this masterpiece for real money.

Okay, maybe I'll test it for a month first.

Reflection of the Day:

When you automate the annoying parts of life, you free up space for things that actually matter.

17th Feb 2025

A few days ago, I got some routine blood work done, and the results were, well... predictable. As expected, my iron levels were dangerously low. I've always been a little anaemic, so this wasn't new to me. I had managed for years on low reserves, but with age, those depleted levels had started to make their presence felt.

I wasn't shocked though. Not with the daily blood-boiling situations I deal with.

See, my family has this adorable habit of trivialising things that, in my world, are critical life issues.

Like when my kids treat my freshly upholstered sofa like a napkin, wiping their greasy little fingers on it as if it's a luxury paper towel.

While I'm raging inside, ready to start a war, they tell me to relax and take a chill pill.

So, off I went to the gynaecologist, hoping for a quick fix, a magic pill to refill my iron reserves and make me less faint-y. But of course, she wanted me to do more tests and come back later.

Now, in my head, I was already trying to figure out when exactly this was going to fit into my life.

Is it that I genuinely don't have time for my own health, or have I just placed myself at the bottom of the priority list?

Honestly, I don't even want to know the answer to that.

This week, though, I was only responsible for one child, thanks to Aliza being away on her school trip.

So, in the precious window of temporary freedom, where I had mapped out my entire week, I had to sacrifice a body massage to squeeze in this medical chore.

Because, of course, health trumps relaxation any day.

But why do these boring adult responsibilities always creep in like weeds, ruining my perfectly good self-care plans?

Later, I finally managed to catch up on my evening walk with my gang of girls, something I'd been missing for ages thanks to my staff crisis.

As expected, we ended up at the same local club we always go to. But these walks are less about fitness and more about therapy.

(Read: long venting sessions about the daily circus of motherhood, including the eternal struggle of getting kids to bed on time.)

I used to watch my mom go for her evening walks, almost religiously. Back then, I thought it was simply her exercise routine. But now I understand. It wasn't just about getting her steps in, or whatever the 10K steps version was in those days. She went out to unload, to vent, to laugh with her girlfriends.

I remember groups of women walking in clusters of twos and threes, chatting away. I'm sure she was complaining about us kids, or discussing some new health hack. But really, it was her way of holding on to her sanity.

And I get it now. I do the same. I go out, talk nonsense with my gang of girls, and we just laugh. Call it therapy if you want. Having your own circle of women, you can call your own is as essential now as it was back then.

Walking with my girls keeps me from losing my mind, and it burns a few calories while we're at it.

Reflection of the day:

Plan for tomorrow - Accidently spill *haldi doodh* on my children's favourite things.

18th Feb 2025

Remember when I said I was getting a Dyson vacuum cleaner to make my staff's life easier? Well, I had gone ahead and ordered it on Amazon, because clearly, I haven't learnt my lesson from the last four times I bought expensive electronics online and found them defective on arrival. What made me think this time would be any different?

The Dyson arrived, and of course, it didn't work. I spent half my morning trying to convince Amazon customer care that I needed a replacement. But Amazon didn't become a billion-dollar company by making things easy. Their policy was clear, if the item was damaged, they would replace it. If it was defective? That was my problem. I had to contact Dyson directly. What a clever little trick to dodge responsibility.

By this point, I was furious. I argued, I reasoned, and when that didn't work, I swore in every language I knew. If Jeh had been around, he would have only been further convinced that his wife had the mouth of a truck driver.

Eventually, I called Dyson's customer representative team, and thankfully, they were slightly more reasonable. After what felt like an interrogation, they agreed to replace the product. Just like that, my blood pressure returned to normal, and I could finally get on with my day.

Rumi came back from school today, and while I had thoroughly enjoyed my little vacation yesterday, meaning, only being responsible for one child instead of two while Aliza was off on her school trip to Goa, today felt different.

The house felt too quiet. It wasn't peaceful or relaxing; rather, it was unsettling.

Rumi may not be the calmest child, but at eight years old, she's still in that phase where she hasn't fully realised, she can defy me yet. I'm making the most of these last pre-teen years while she still believes I know everything and doesn't argue just for sport. She has her moments of defiance, but we haven't reached the daily battle stage yet.

With Aliza, it's a different story. The moment she walks in from school, we're arguing about something. Her screen time, her missing homework, her sudden dislike for vegetables, why wearing a jacket in winter is "not a vibe." That noise is what makes the house feel alive.

Without her at home, there is no door-slamming or loud arguments. Just... silence.

And I don't like it one bit.

Later at night, after tucking Rumi into bed, Jeh and I slumped in front of the TV and watched *Rocky aur Rani ki Prem Kahaani*. We both love mindless, over-the-top cinema, which has no logic, but is pure entertainment.

At some point, we started talking about how our own lives weren't too different from Rocky and Rani's.

We grew up in completely different worlds. Different parts of India, different religion, food, mother tongues. Jeh spent his childhood listening to songs from ABBA, while I was singing Raj Kapoor songs with my grandparents. He grew up eating roast chicken, while I was raised on *dal chawal*. Even our upbringings were poles apart, yet somehow, we just fit together.

And while Jeh was busy enjoying the movie, I was falling in love with Alia Bhatt's lehenga. If I ever got married again (to the same man, hopefully), I would wear exactly that. Except I never even got to wear a lehenga at my own wedding.

I wore a sari. A beautiful sari, sure, but not my tradition, not what I had imagined. And the worst part? I never even questioned it.

I was young and went along with it. Because that's how women are wired, right? We are taught to adjust, accommodate, and fit into the husband's family traditions without ever questioning it.

And now that I think about it, why did I not speak up? Was I trying to impress my new family by conforming? Why did I not say that it's my wedding too and I want to wear what I want. I mean, it's a small thing, but also not a small thing.

I'd like to blame conditioning, this silent subtle messaging that tells us to compromise before we even realize we're compromising. Otherwise, what else could it be?

And as this deep revelation dawned on me, I looked at Jeh blissfully unaware of my internal monologue, laughing away.

Reflection of the day:

It starts small. A lehenga, a decision, a choice we let go of without questioning. And before we know it, we've trained ourselves to make space for everyone else but ourselves.

Time to speak up.

19th Feb 2025

Nothing exciting today. I had planned a nice, long full-body massage since I had more time with Aliza not around. But of course, instead of being pampered, I ended up getting poked for more blood tests. Just my luck.

But the "highlight" of my day was becoming a barber. Now, Jeh's barber isn't just any barber. He's a charity project Jeh refuses to give up on. Apparently, now that the guy is married, Jeh feels even more responsible for his livelihood. Sweet, except for one problem, the man cannot cut hair to save his life. Every time Jeh gets a trim, it looks like a DIY experiment.

I've been telling him to go to a proper salon, but he won't hear of it. Today, after some serious nagging, he agreed to dye his hair a little but on one condition: I had to do it, while the barber stood there watching, getting paid for absolutely nothing.

At this rate, I wouldn't be surprised if Jeh wanted to install a salon station at home so he never has to step out for a haircut again. He genuinely believes he's living in India of the 1950s, where all services should be done at home instead of being outsourced.

Later in the evening, my dear friend dropped by. Our kids go to the same school, and like me, she was also temporarily promoted to parenting just one child since our older ones were away on the school trip.

We were both basking in the sheer joy of not having to play referee between siblings or listen to endless debates about who stole whose pencil five years ago.

Since her younger one is besties with Rumi, we decided to combine our blessings and set up a playdate, followed by an early dinner. While the kids ran around, burning off their endless energy, we sat there, comparing notes on how efficiently we had maximised our limited-time offer of single-child parenting.

At the end of the conversation, we were both wondering if we should start a petition for staggered school trips, one child gone at a time, all year round.

Reflection of the Day:

If bad haircuts build character, Jeh might be the most evolved man I know.

20th Feb 2025

Have you ever seen *Kabhi Khushi Kabhie Gham*? You know that iconic scene where Jaya Bachchan stands at the door, *thali* in hand, waiting for Shah Rukh Khan? Well, today, I was Jaya Bachchan. No *thali* in hand, but the emotions were all there.

Aliza was returning from her school trip. It was only four days, but it felt like four years. I'd gotten used to my mini vacation of handling just one kid, but I also missed her more than I'd admit. I woke up feeling like it was Eid, Diwali, and Christmas rolled into one, made all her favourite food, and cleaned her room like every other mom waiting for her child's approval.

Meanwhile, Rumi decided that a simple "Welcome Back" note wouldn't be enough. Instead, she dedicated hours to crafting a masterpiece of sibling love with glitter, stickers and layers of folded paper. For all their fights, I knew she had missed her sister deeply. Every night, she'd go into her big sister's room and subtly ask me, "When is she back?" while pretending not to care. These two fight over the last piece of chocolate like sworn enemies, but at the core, they are each other's biggest support systems.

Later in the evening, Jeh (my husband, but more accurately, my third child) had a dentist appointment. Naturally, he insisted I come along. This man is a fully grown adult with a business and a driver's license, yet the thought of sitting in a dentist's chair alone is unacceptable.

Now, here's the funny part: the dentist's clinic happens to be in the same building as Starbucks, which I have previously ranted about, especially when Aliza tags along, always trying to convince me to buy her a sugar-loaded drink. But today was different. With no kids nagging, Jeh and I turned this dentist visit into a coffee date. If you're picturing a cute, romantic outing, please don't. This was less of a "date" and more of two tired parents caffeinating themselves and zoning out.

But then I remembered that Rumi had finished her class, and we called her to meet us. In an attempt to act like a cool mom, I ordered her a chocolate drink. She was stunned and kept looking at me to see if it was some trick. But then, when she realised that I was the mom who had made spontaneous Starbucks dreams come true, she got super thrilled.

From Starbucks, we headed straight to the airport, buzzing with anticipation. Standing at the arrivals gate, we did what all parents do, we scanned every face, every step, waiting for our child to walk through.

And then, there she was. The moment we saw Aliza, grinning from ear to ear, we knew she had had the best time ever. And in that second, all our overthinking, all our questions (Did she miss us? Did she eat properly? Did she get enough sleep?) disappeared.

Because every parent knows that look, that "I had an amazing time, but I'm also happy to be home" face. And that was enough. Because our happiness is directly wired to theirs. So, even though she was the one who had just returned from Goa, we were probably more excited than she was.

Reflection of the Day

Parenting is the biggest juxtaposition there is. You spend half your time wishing for a break and the other half missing your kids so much it physically hurts.

21th Feb 2025

Aliza had barely stepped foot inside the house the previous night when she demanded her phone back. It was as if she had just returned from a tech detox retreat against her will, and now, she wasn't planning on wasting a second. From the moment she got it, her fingers and the screen became inseparable. If phones gave out awards for loyalty, hers would have handed her a trophy right then and there.

When she woke up the next morning, which was actually noon, her phone was still the first thing she saw. She put on her favourite Taylor Swift songs and stared at the screen without blinking, as if Taylor herself was about to step out and give her a private concert.

It was already hard enough to accept that she was waking up so late, but seeing her glued to her phone the moment she opened her eyes was affecting me on so many levels. It wasn't just about the excessive screen time, it was bad for her eyes, focus, and concentration, and I couldn't help but wonder what kind of content she was consuming.

The worst part was that I couldn't even say anything. She had just returned from a trip where she had been away from her phone for four days, so any attempt to stop her or take it away would have been unfair. I had to summon every ounce of self-control to go against my instincts and let her be.

Once she finally acknowledged the real world, something heartwarming happened. She brought out presents. This was historic because teenagers are not exactly known for thinking about others while on trips. Yet, here she was, handing me dark chocolate, not just any random souvenir, but something she knew I loved. She remembered that her mom always had a soft spot for dark chocolate, especially the antioxidant-rich kind that made me feel healthy while eating junk. In my mind, if there's any food with the word antioxidant attached to it, I will eat it.

Rumi was equally thrilled when she saw that her *Didi* had not forgotten her. For someone who acted indifferent toward her big sister most of the time, the joy on her face was undeniable. Sure, the gift was nice, but she was more thrilled from knowing she was acknowledged by Aliza. That was huge for her.

With the gift-giving ceremony done, the unpacking began. Clothes, shoes, and snack wrappers tumbled out of her bags, covering every surface in sight. It made me question if she had gone on a four-day school trip or moved out entirely.

By the time we wrapped up the unpacking, it was finally dinner time. It was a perfect meal, where everyone was actually present, and no one was secretly scrolling under the table. Aliza shared all her Goa trip stories, and once again, the house felt complete again.

Since it was the weekend, Jeh and I went out to meet our friends, leaving the kids at home. They swore on every holy book in existence that they would sleep on time. But the moment we walked back in, the house ratted them out. The TV was warm, the remote was missing from its usual place, and there were crumbled snack packets lying around, not even hidden, just abandoned in their hurry to switch everything off and pretend they had been asleep for hours.

But I let it go.

Reflection of the day:

Sometimes, being selectively blind is the secret to maintaining a good relationship with your children.

22nd Feb 2025

Lazy morning. I woke up late because last night's scene with friends had stretched beyond a reasonable hour, and now, at nearly 40, sleep deprivation really messes with me. It's not like in our twenties, when we could function on four hours of sleep and still conquer the world. These days, losing even an hour of sleep feels like life's out to get me.

Barely made it to the dining table when the kids erupted into World War III, screaming and fighting like Russia and Ukraine over something entirely insignificant. I swear, if they weren't my kids, I would have said such mean things to them. But since I am, in fact, their mother and responsible for their overall well-being, I had to step in as the chief peace negotiator before things escalated.

Anyway, let's talk about our dog, who, by the way, is the cutest creature on this planet. I say this with complete bias because, despite never being a dog person and never growing up with one, I have somehow become ridiculously attached to this little furball. The decision to get him was not made lightly. Years of debating and contemplating responsibilities finally led us to take the plunge, all for the kids, obviously. I had read somewhere that dogs are great for children's emotional and mental health, and you know me and my health, if you tell me something is good for the body or brain, I am all in, just like my obsession with antioxidants.

The moment we brought him home, Aliza claimed him as her heart and soul. Rumi, on the other hand, took her sweet time warming up, acting like he was a stranger who had overstayed his welcome. But now, she can't live without him. In fact, none of us can. He is thoroughly spoilt and is treated like royalty. He sleeps in Aliza's room, which he has unilaterally declared as his kingdom. He is never left outside or ignored, always included, and definitely one of us.

So today was bath day, which in our house is a full-scale operation. Jeh, who is a hands-on dad, is also a hands-on dog dad, so he insists on bathing him himself. Aliza, being the affectionate dog mom, she claims to be, always promises to help. But she is also 13, which means promises are as solid as air, and today was no different. Jeh asked for her help, she conveniently forgot, and the next thing I knew, an argument had broken out.

Now, here's the thing about Jeh, he can handle a lot of things, but if he ever has friction with the kids, he just cannot handle it. And guess who became his default punching bag? Me, of course.

And then, suddenly, I was at the receiving end too. And the worst part is that I did NOTHING. Not a single thing. But utter four words in response, and boom, he was mad at me too. And since I am the eternal peacekeeper, I had to keep quiet and smooth things over, which sucked.

Why do we have to take this nonsense just to keep the peace? I know Jeh wasn't actually upset with me, he was mad at Aliza. But why does that make it okay to redirect his frustration onto me? I'm also human, no? But I'm also a wife. And a woman. So apparently, I have to take it.

Moving on to later, Rumi finally agreed to do her homework after what felt like an all-you-can-watch TV buffet. It was a long math worksheet, and naturally, she wanted to know why on earth schools loved torturing kids with so many problems. Since I had to sound like a responsible parent, I explained that the more she practiced, the better she'd get. But honestly, I sometimes wonder if teachers secretly enjoy making parents suffer by sending home these never-ending worksheets.

She was learning long division for the first time, and I somehow managed to explain it to her without her losing interest or temper.

Reflection of the day:

Keeping a child engaged in math without tears and tantrums is some next-level parenting achievement.

23rd Feb 2025

You know it's going to be a great, maybe even historic, Sunday when there's an India vs Pakistan cricket match in the evening. It's practically a national event. But more on that later.

The day started with Aliza's drama class, which had been a source of stress for her all week, or so she claimed. Given how much she had been talking about being nervous for her drama exam, I expected her to be in full panic mode on the way to class. But no. My 13-year-old was chilling. Singing along to her favourite music, completely zen, like she was on a joyride, not on her way to face her so-called fears.

There was a lesson in this, and I was a little torn. On one hand, I wanted her to stress just a tiny bit, so she would take things seriously, be prepared, and do her work on time. But on the other hand, here she was at thirteen, already having cracked the code of life. Stressing wasn't going to help her. Staying calm, collected, and living in the moment was. I admired that. Truly. It's something we adults could learn from.

Don't we spend half our lives living in the future, trying to stay one step ahead so we don't fall behind in this circus called life? And then the other half in the past, replaying scenes we wish we could undo. Every wise person, every spiritual teacher, keeps saying the same thing: the present is where life actually happens. A meaningful life exists only in the now. And yet this exact thing feels like the hardest to do. This is what creates anxiety, fear, stress and every heavy feeling we carry.

So, there I was, thinking I was teaching my daughter something, when actually I was the one learning from her. She keeps telling me I am a fake follower of Brahma Kumaris and Eckhart Tolle. I read their books, I love their teachings, I talk about them. The only problem is that I don't always manage to practice them.

But here was the lesson, sitting right in front of me, eating dinner in my house every night. My own child. Living the philosophy, I keep trying so hard to practice. How could I not see it.

Later in the evening, I forced the family into some screen-free bonding time by suggesting a few rounds of UNO and Boggle. It was my way of keeping everyone, including my husband away from their devices. At first, they played along. But after a couple of rounds, Aliza looked at me and declared Boggle as a super boring game. And that was an epiphany for me.

When I was her age, Boggle was peak entertainment. We had no Netflix, no iPhones, no iPads, and no endless supply of YouTube shorts to fry our brains. We actually had patience for things. But this generation has consumed too much already. Unless something doesn't flash or beep, it's not worth their time.

Thankfully, UNO saved the day. That's the one game they love, especially when playing against their dad, because for them, defeating him is a sport in itself.

After the games, we sat down to watch the match, and the excitement was solid. But the actual match wasn't happening on the cricket field, it was me vs bedtime. Because no matter how thrilling the match was, Monday morning existed, and school wasn't going to care that India was playing with Pakistan. Of course, my kids had zero intention of sleeping early, and getting them into bed was a lost cause.

Reflection of the day:

Parenting is basically trying to enforce rules while your kids pretend, they don't exist.

24th Feb 2025

You know how I keep complaining about Aliza always being late? Yeah, well, today she outdid herself. Broke her own record. Set a new personal best in tardiness. Though it was technically my fault.

I'm the human alarm clock in this house, and today, I malfunctioned. Woke up a little later than usual, which meant the kids woke up late, which meant Aliza had a solid excuse to pin all her lateness on me.

Meanwhile, my sweet little baby girl Rumi got ready in no time, marched downstairs, and was at the bus stop like a responsible student. But Aliza? Oh no. She was just getting started on packing her bag according to her timetable, something I've told her a million times to do the night before. But why listen to Mom when you can live life on the edge, right?

And then, the school bus arrived. Rumi got on. Aliza was still running around. The bus driver waited. And waited. And waited. Until even he gave up and drove off.

Now, Aliza was panicking. I was panicking. Even the walls of the house seemed to be panicking. I called the bus driver frantically begging and promising my eternal gratitude. He gave me 8 minutes to get to the next stop.

Aliza and I jumped into the car, racing against time and against traffic. And just as the bus came into sight, we started chasing it, waving like maniacs, hoping someone inside sees us.

Finally, after what felt like an entire lifetime, someone, probably an angel in the form of a student, saw us. The bus stopped. Aliza, finally got on.

Now, I was hoping this ordeal would teach her a lesson. Maybe she'd start waking up on time? Pack her bag the night before? Develop some kind of urgency? Nope. Absolutely not. Fast forward a few hours, and she's late for an online class while I'm hyperventilating because her teacher has once again told me off. But Aliza doesn't seem to budge. I swear, she's got some kind of immunity to urgency.

At this point, I just know my blood pressure spiked today.

While the kids were at school in the morning, I checked up on our farm and office construction where things are not going as per plan. But this was more calming and I needed some distraction to bring my morning cortisol spike down.

Oh, and speaking of distractions, remember how I said I have full control over my kitchen decisions? It's empowering. And today was the day I went shopping for kitchen essentials.

And while I was standing in the *bartan ki dukaan*, I realised I have become my mother- an aunty.

I caught myself freaking out over white bowls. White bowls. Beautiful, sleek, elegant, perfectly matching white bowls. I could barely contain myself. There I was, surrounded by blenders and dinner sets and it didn't make sense to feel this wave of excitement that I usually do when I score the last piece of a dress in my size at a sale at Zara.

I stood there, clutching these bowls, realising that I have evolved. I am now a person who experiences pure joy over ceramic tableware. And I'm actually okay with it.

Reflection of the Day:

Chasing a school bus at top speed is not a sustainable cardio routine.

25th Feb 2025

My parents were taking the evening flight to come in to see us. The kids were thrilled, my parents were thrilled, and I... Well, I was secretly looking forward to finally sleeping in while my mom took over the morning school prep. A well-deserved break, if you ask me.

I'd spent the entire morning basking in happy thoughts of my parents' arrival later in the day. Then Rumi came home from school and had a full-blown meltdown. And it took only a few seconds to turn my happy thoughts into a feeling of dread. Our house help had washed her beloved stuffed toy. The one she sleeps with. Every. Single. Night. But logic and grief don't go hand in hand when you're eight.

Apparently, the washing had made it "too hard," and she was fuming. But the irony was that it had been washed with love, all because our dog had gotten a little too affectionate with it earlier. But no, that logic didn't fly with my emotionally devastated child. She was heartbroken and absolutely hilarious.

It reminded me of when my older daughter was little and her biggest problem in life was that she was convinced monkeys would steal her chocolates. No one else, just monkeys. You know, normal childhood fears. It's so endearing to see what counts as a catastrophe when you're a kid. It just makes you love them more or at least love their innocence more.

We picked my parents up from the airport, and, as expected, the kids wasted zero time making elaborate plans with their grandparents, especially with their *Nanu*. Plans that were basically a direct assault on my parenting rules: more junk food, more screen time, no homework, and just a general disregard for Mom's authority.

But I didn't want to stand in the way of this. They don't get to see each other that often, so I let it slide. And then, the sweetest thing happened. Rumi crawled into bed with them and declared she was sleeping there for the night. That was just so sweet. I wasn't surprised, though. My father becomes a child with my kids and plays with them like that. And the kids simply love it. No wonder Rumi wanted to spend every single second with her *Nanu* while he was here.

Reflection of the Day:

Grandparents wipe out all your rules in a matter of minutes, and the kids love them even more for it.

26th Feb 2025

Holidays are supposed to be relaxing. That's what they sell you. But with my parents, a holiday means packing in so many activities that by the end, I need another holiday just to recover.

The day started with shopping, where *Nanu* transformed into a human ATM who believes in pure indulgence when it comes to his grandchildren. There was no spending limit and no budgeting. Rumi's dreams were coming true as anything she pointed at became hers, and Aliza was gravitating toward more expensive items she knew Mumma would never buy her. I stood there, pretending to be in control while silently calculating how much damage had already been done.

Lunch was at a place known for its food, and it didn't disappoint. With everyone ordering something different, the table soon turned into a grand spread, like a mini buffet just for us. Afterwards, we went to the farmhouse, my parents' future retirement home in their minds. The second they stepped in; I could see them making plans.

My dad was already imagining long, thoughtful walks and peaceful afternoons, and my mom looked ready to launch into full-time farming.

And then, it happened. Something so bizarre yet so familiar.

My father, a man who has never expressed strong emotions over food, was standing next to a mulberry plant, plucking and eating berries straight from the branch with the serious concentration of a man solving world problems. A few days ago, Jeh had done the exact same thing, carefully selecting each mulberry as if he were inspecting diamonds under a magnifying glass.

I think this is a family-wide male obsession. I am convinced that Jeh and my father must have had a discussion about the superiority of hand-picked mulberries versus store-bought ones.

My mother and Rumi were on a harvesting rampage, gathering vegetables like they were running their own farm-to-table restaurant. On the other side, *Nanu* and Aliza had spread out a mat, lay down, and completely checked out from life without a care in the world. They were staring at the sky as if they were narrating a BBC nature documentary. It was 5 PM. The only thing above them was a mildly interesting crow.

Watching all of them do what they loved made me realise something, I did not randomly wake up one day and decide to be obsessed with clean food and organic eating. This is deeply embedded in my DNA.

When we got home, my mom was overjoyed to cook with her freshly picked vegetables. The whole farm-to-table experience was giving her an almost childlike happiness. Jeh and the kids, meanwhile, just watched quietly, beginning to understand where my obsession with clean, natural food really came from. For once, I didn't have to explain anything.

Growing up, my grandfather always bought fruits and vegetables himself to make sure the family got the best produce. He believed in home remedies and Ayurveda, never in allopathy, and often called packaged foods "rubbish wrapped in shiny packets." My mom carried that same mindset. She made us homemade face packs, relied on age-old Ayurvedic tricks, and cared for us with the same wisdom she had learnt from her mother, my *Nani*.

By the time we wrapped up dinner, I realised we had accomplished something incredible, the kids had gone an entire day without screens and had actually connected with nature. This is gold-medal-level parenting for sure.

I know I have a one-track mind when it comes to my kids' health and food, but that just means I am a good mom.

Reflection of the day:

My kids think farm-fresh veggies are a personality trait, too bad their actual personality is refusing to eat them.

27th Feb 2025

This morning felt like a mass departure, my dad left on the morning flight to Delhi, Jeh headed to work, the kids rushed off to school, and suddenly, it was just me and my mom. And we made plans.

The day was pure mother-daughter time: Mummy *ke haath ka khana*, guilt-free shopping, endless cups of chai, and mindless chit-chat. It felt like such a special day having my mom, just to myself, without any of her daily responsibilities. And what a contrast, while my 13-year-old actively avoids me like I carry a contagious mom virus, here I am, nearly 40, clinging to every second with my mother. I don't get to see her often, and when I do, I turn into a clingy, overgrown toddler.

For once, I got to just be the child instead of the mom. No one claiming to be starving five minutes after lunch, no one demanding that I mediate a sibling fight over something as non-trivial as who breathed too loudly.

When the kids came home, my mom took over like a seasoned pro, handling tantrums and fulfilling demands with the patience of a saint. Once they were sent off to their evening classes, my mom and I went to Starbucks. Now, I know, I know, I have ranted about this coffee chain before, but it was the closest option, and convenience always wins. So yes, Starbucks and I are in a toxic love-hate relationship, but today, it served its purpose.

In the evening, Jeh casually asked if I wanted to step out to meet friends. The true question was whether I wanted an evening of fun, knowing I could wake up late because my mom was there to handle the morning madness. The answer was a resounding YES.

My mother, who has spent her entire life in service to her family, willingly took over yet again, even after 40+ married years of relentless dedication. It's commendable, and completely beyond my capabilities. I know for a fact I do not have that level of sacrifice in me.

The night was relaxing but super, super late. I ended up catching up with a long-lost friend, and it was unexpectedly special. She was one of my first few friends in this town, but we had lost touch over the years. And now, here we were, reconnecting in our adult lives, looking back at how life had panned out for us.

Reflection of the Day:

Once a mom is always a mom, thankfully caffeine helps to survive this.

28th Feb 2025

Some people go shopping for clothes, others for gadgets. I, however, go shopping for kitchen essentials because, according to my mom, my kitchen was woefully unequipped. It turns out there is a long list of things I had no idea were necessary in a functioning kitchen. But my mom, being the culinary superstar that she is, took charge and decided to rescue my kitchen from its state of neglect. I found myself nodding along as she filled the cart with things I couldn't even name. There was a very specific ginger grater which I thought I didn't need, but I didn't dare question it. She kept tossing things into the cart as gracefully as someone plucking flowers, and I just followed her, leaving my brain somewhere behind. After this endless round of shopping, which I believed would make my kitchen ready for a MasterChef competition, we finally paid the hefty bill. I was just glad to leave, because I honestly could not take learning about another kitchen tool today.

From there, it was straight to a doctor's visit for my mom. She has some health concerns, and while her regular doctors have reassured her that everything is fine, I needed to hear it myself. It's a strange transition when you start worrying about your parents the way they once worried about you. I've been paranoid about their health for a while now, constantly double-checking, and insisting on second opinions. It's taken me time to accept that they are getting older, but I still have this irrational belief that if I stay on top of things, I can somehow pause the ageing process. Thankfully, everything checked out fine, and I could breathe a little easier, until the next health concern, of course.

After all that, we decided we deserved some relaxation, which meant a trip to the salon. A nice, long hair wash was non-negotiable, mainly, because after visiting a hospital, I have this urgent need to scrub myself from head to toe as if I've picked up every possible germ lurking in the air. The hospital smell clings, and I need it off me. So, this salon visit was actually for sanitary purposes.

By the time we got home, I was officially done for the day. I told Jeh he was on full kid duty because my mom and I had been running around since morning, and we needed a break. Especially her, she's not exactly young anymore, and, well, neither am I. I'm turning 40 this year and as a child I thought 40 was almost retirement age. And I still think like that child. Plus, Jeh and I had to head out to a birthday party at night, and he knows me well enough to understand that if I didn't get some rest beforehand, I'd be cranky. And no one, no one, wants that.

The night out followed its usual pattern of being fun and going on till late. We ate far more than necessary, with me declaring every bite a "special occasion," while conveniently ignoring the fact that every night out somehow becomes one. Thankfully, I don't drink, so the only consequence the next morning is exhaustion rather than a hangover.

Reflection of the Day:

Watching my parents age is tough, but watching my mom outwork me in my own kitchen is downright humiliating.

1st March 2025

My mom wasn't the only one who consulted the doctor yesterday. I figured it was time to address my own mysterious symptoms too. For some time now, I've been having dizzy spells where I feel like I'm about to faint but never actually do. It's like my body enjoys creating suspense but refuses to follow through. The doctor, as expected, had ordered a few tests. Jeh decided to take me this morning, not out of any grand romantic gesture, but because my mom had more exciting plans lined up.

And that worked perfectly for both of us.

While I was busy pretending not to be scared of needles, my mom had taken on a much bigger mission, ensuring that my kids contributed significantly to the mall's monthly revenue. They had already gone shopping with *Nanu*, yet somehow, their wardrobes, toy and book collections and needs in general were still lacking something critical. My mother, funnily, saw no reason to deny them. Off they went, determined to cover every store they might have missed the first time.

Since it was a Saturday and there was no school to get in the way of their grand plans, my kids took full advantage of *Nani's* generosity. With my mom leaving the next day, they knew this was their last chance before their corporate sponsor packed up and left.

By lunchtime, we all reunited at home. After a meal that I barely remember because I was still recovering from the morning's blood tests, my mom and I headed out for another one of her must-do activities, a visit to a *jyotish.* Some people explore new restaurants or historical landmarks when they visit another city. My mom finds astrologers. If there's one within a reasonable distance, she will track them down. At this point, I've stopped questioning it. It's a tradition.

Dinner was, without a doubt, the most important event of the day. Since this was our last meal together before she left, my mom went all out. Not a single person in our house eats non-veg when she is around, not because she stops us, but because she makes vegetarian food so well that even the biggest meat lovers wouldn't dare refuse. Tonight, she had prepared a North Indian *chaat* feast that could make even the most passionate butter chicken fan temporarily forget about chicken altogether.

There were crispy *papdis*, perfectly spiced *aloo tikkis*, tangy *chutneys*, and melt-in-your-mouth *dahi bhallas.* It was such an emotional experience for me, taking me back to my childhood.

After stuffing ourselves to the point of regret, it was time for bed. I curled up next to my mom, feeling full and happy. Rumi, never one to miss an opportunity, decided to poke fun at me.

"*Mumma, you're so old, and you still want to cuddle your mom?*" she said, with a very cute smirk on her face.

But if she thought that was an insult, she was mistaken.

"If you can sleep with your mumma, then I can sleep with mine," I shot back. "*Age has nothing to do with it.*" She responded by giving me a loving smile this time.

Reflection of the Day:

No matter how grown up you pretend to be, nothing beats the comfort of your mom's food or cuddles.

2nd March 2025

Mummy flew back in the late afternoon, but not before leaving behind a food memory that will stay with us for days. She made *dal baati choorma*. This meal should come with a health warning, given how rich and indulgent it is. I always find myself reaching for another helping because it's always a limited time offer for me. Being away in another city, I find myself constantly thinking about my mom's food. I think I'm mostly craving that familiar plate which tastes like home.

Anyway, moving on, *baati*, for the uninitiated, is *roti* taken to extreme levels of indulgence. A dense, baked ball of wheat flour, sometimes stuffed with spiced mashed potatoes. Basically, its carbs within carbs. Once it's out of the oven, it gets dunked in *ghee*. The accompanying dal is a thick, aromatic blend of lentils, mildly nutritious but only until you pour another spoonful of ghee on top.

And then, there's *choorma*. If *baati* wasn't enough, *choorma is baati*'s sweeter, slightly more sinful cousin. It starts as crumbled, deep-fried dough, which is drenched in sugar and *ghee* in the next step. It tests self-discipline, if you ask me.

Since she's Rajasthani, this is second nature to her. But if I even thought about making something this elaborate, I'd need two days of mental preparation, two days to cook, and another two to recover. She, on the other hand, made it before we even woke up. I don't know where she gets the energy from, but I'd like a fraction of it.

Since she was leaving today, I wanted to pamper her a little. Over the last few days, she had completely taken over my kitchen, spoilt my kids, and done enough shopping to single-handedly boost the economy. A little salon time felt like the least I could do. So, we went for facials and a good head oil massage. I hoped it would relax her a bit, maybe even slow her down for a while. But my mother is built differently. She walked out of the salon looking fresher than ever and with more energy than before. Clearly, she operates on a different fuel system than the rest of us.

We had a huge task waiting for us at home. Mummy had been shopping for very odd things, like a particular type of red peanuts she insists are not available in Delhi. And there were several things like that. Now the challenge was to fit everything into one suitcase and keep it under 15 kgs. The rest of us looked at the overflowing pile and knew this was impossible. But my mom, like all Indian moms, has a special skill set when it comes to packing. She rearranged, folded, stuffed, and sat on the suitcase until the zip finally closed. It was hilarious to watch, and I even clicked a picture. Honestly, I don't know how she does it, but I feel like if NASA put her in charge of loading spaceships, astronauts would never run out of supplies.

After lunch, we drove to the airport. The car ride was a mix of instructions, reminders, unsolicited advice, what to cook, how to store vegetables properly, why I should drink *haldi doodh*, and a quick lecture on how my sleep schedule is ruining my health. She was cramming in a lifetime of motherly guidance into the 30-minute drive. The lecture went on until we hugged her goodbye, and she walked towards the departure area.

And then, out of nowhere, I felt a tear roll down my cheek. I hadn't expected it. I mean, we talk all the time, but there's something about seeing her leave that always stings. Maybe it's the realisation that no matter how old I get, having my mom around still feels like a safety net, a comforting presence that makes everything feel easier.

To digest the absurd amount of *dal baati choorma* I had consumed, I drove straight to the club for a walk after dropping her off. But the walk wasn't just about the food. It was also a way to distract myself from that tiny ache that came from watching my mom go back to her own home after spending days making mine feel even more like one.

Reflection of the Day:

Moms leave, but their love, and at least one bag of things you didn't ask for always stay behind.

3rd March 2025

Got a reality check this morning that made me stare at the ceiling for a long time, long enough to gather the strength to get out of bed. I had spent the last few days in a blissful bubble, pushing aside all responsibilities under the noble excuse of "family time". But today, there was no running away. Everything I had ignored was waiting for me, arms crossed, tapping its foot impatiently.

First on the list, office construction. Now, I am usually quite proactive with this, but the thing about vendors and contractors is that their concept of time is completely different from the rest of us. Things that were promised "by next week" are still in the same state three months later. Normally, this would boil my blood, but while my parents were in town, I had made a conscious decision to not let it bother me. Priorities, right? Spending time with them mattered more than chasing after delayed deadlines. But now that they had left, it was time to face the reality.

Then there was the farm construction. I love the idea of having a farm, but every time I get a new update about something being "almost done" but not quite, I realise that my patience is on life support. I had put this on hold for a few days, but today, the follow-ups had to happen.

Somewhere between trying to manage two never-ending construction projects, I had to write my book. A book I am passionate about, but some days, writing feels like staring at a blank page while my brain refuses to participate. Today was one of those days.

And then there were the kids. Oh, the kids. Their homework had officially piled up to dangerous levels, and I was the lucky person tasked with making sure they actually did it.

And, when I thought I was making some progress, I realised that both the kids' exams were just 10 days away. Exams. The word alone sends shivers down my spine. Not because I am writing them, but because kids' exams are a full-time job for parents. The planning and the revision schedules, and that's just me, forget the kids.

So today wasn't just about catching up on tasks. It was a harsh reality check that no matter how much you avoid things, they will still be waiting for you when you return, except now, they are even messier and more urgent.

Reflection of the Day:

Life waits for no one... except my kids, who seem to believe exams can be prepared for in a single night.

4th March 2025

Today was the much-awaited "show my reports to the doctor" day, and the verdict was in, I had *dimaag ki bimari*. Or as doctors like to call it, anxiety.

Jeh had stayed back specifically to witness this confirmation with his own ears. He had been convinced for a while now that my dizzy, near-fainting spells were just my overactive brain playing games with me. And sure enough, the doctor backed him up. Except, turns out, it wasn't just anxiety, but nerve compression that was the real culprit. And the solution was nutritional supplements for nerve health and, as expected, anti-anxiety pills.

Now, I'm no doctor, but I used my own highly logical reasoning here. If nutritional supplements were going to fix the issue, then why would I need the anxiety pills? My anxiety only kicks in when I feel like I'm about to faint, so no fainting = no anxiety. Simple. So, I decided to skip the anti-anxiety pills altogether and trust that my nerves would sort themselves out.

Since we got done at the doctor's quickly, miraculously avoiding the usual waiting game, Jeh and I found ourselves with extra time. Jeh glanced at me, half-smiling. "So...lunch?" he said. And just like that, our morning chore turned into something nicer.

Now, Jeh's idea of a lunch date is finding another excuse to drink coffee. We went to a coffee shop he is deeply, emotionally invested in. If he could, he'd probably start funding it just to ensure their coffee quality never drops. His love for coffee is next-level. A coffee snob in the truest sense, one of those people who can taste a cup and immediately declare whether the beans were sourced from Ethiopia, Colombia, or someone's backyard.

After fuelling ourselves, we moved on to the next task, which was inspecting the dining table for our farm before it was dispatched. Simple enough, right? Wrong. We got to the shop and saw the table in all its glory, except for one major issue. The legs were so close together that instead of looking like a dining table, it seemed like a piece of modern art that nobody understands.

He tried to convince us that it was a "design feature," while we tried to convince him that we'd rather not have our guests feel like they were playing musical chairs every time they tried to sit down.

After half an hour of intense negotiation with the shop owner to redo the entire leg design, our mission somewhat got accomplished and I decided to drag Jeh to the office site since he had taken the day off. I needed his input on a few decisions, and after getting there, we realised something major, our office is on the fifth floor, and we hadn't thought about installing safety grills.

It took one good look down from the balcony for us to panic-call the architect and make it his problem immediately. Crisis averted, hopefully.

By the time we got home, the kids were still at their classes, so I took the opportunity to head to the neighbourhood park for an evening walk with a friend. I think there is nothing better than meeting a friend to end the day in a nice and non-stressful way.

Reflection of the Day:

I think I thrive on to-do lists.

5th March 2025

Woke up this morning with the best of intentions. I had set my alarm, laid out my workout gear the night before, and even envisioned a productive, healthy start, involving Pilates and mindfulness.

I rolled out the mat, took a deep breath, and realised almost immediately that my body had other plans. The moment I sat down, everything inside me whispered a very clear no thank you. My muscles felt like they were holding a quiet rebellion and I had no intention of negotiating with them.

The instructor on the screen kept urging everyone to find the stretch and lean into the discomfort. I looked at him, looked at my stubborn hamstrings, and felt nothing except a deep loyalty to the comfort of my bed.

So, I gave up calmly and confidently. I pushed the mat back into its corner and carried on with my day as if I had never even attempted to be that person who does morning stretches. Some days your body just wants peace, not Pilates.

Then came my monthly pilgrimage to Jeh's office, a ritual that has become oddly ceremonial in our household. Jeh likes to call it "Report Card Day," and he does so with all the drama of a headmaster about to announce who passed and who failed. He genuinely believes his company's performance should be reviewed like a school report card.

Anyway, I sat through graphs, numbers and percentages, while nodding at all the right moments. The company did great last month. Gold star for everyone, I guess.

I rushed home hoping for a few minutes to breathe before the evening really began. Instead, I walked straight into our usual family scene. The kids were already home, their bags and shoes flung across the passage in a pattern only they can understand, and half eaten lunch-boxes sitting around like tiny passive-aggressive notes.

Right in the middle of it all lay Apollo, our golden retriever, our third child, spread out on the floor without a care in the world.

I had just started preparing myself for the next round of homework drama and dinner decisions when something unbelievable happened. My phone rang. And not with a spam call offering credit cards. It was the vet. The same vet I had been trying to reach for more than a month. I stared at the screen for a second, almost suspicious, wondering if I was dreaming.

Apollo has been limping for a while now, and it has been sitting heavily on all of us. He is not just our dog, he is the heartbeat of this home, the source of our laughter and fur stuck to our clothes. Usually, he moves around with a level of excitement that makes you wonder if he runs on electricity, sprinting from room to room and greeting us like we have returned from a long voyage even when we only stepped away for a minute.

The past few weeks have been different. He has been slow, unsure on the stairs, lifting his paw every now and then with this confused little look that breaks you in a way nothing else can. We tried everything we could think of. Rest. Warm compresses. Gentle massages. Turmeric, of course, because being Indian means turmeric is our version of duct tape. But nothing worked.

We realised we needed a proper vet. And not just anyone. We needed the one everyone raves about; the one people book months in advance. The one with a waitlist longer than a top college's admission list.

He was our best shot. Mainly because he was local. If he hadn't called back, we would have had no choice but to drive Apollo to another city. And that would've been a logistical disaster. Because road-tripping with Apollo is not an ordinary car ride. He either insists on sitting in my lap, as if he's a poodle and not a golden retriever, or he attempts to co-pilot with Jeh, determined to help drive. Neither scenario is ideal.

So yes, finally securing an appointment with the best vet in our own city felt like winning a lottery.

Reflection of the day:

Survived spreadsheets and scored a vet appointment. Who says I didn't accomplish great things?

6th March 2025

Of course. Just my luck.

The vet messaged early in the morning saying he'd been caught up in an emergency and couldn't see Apollo after all. After a whole month of chasing him, texting and following up, he vanished when the big day arrived. Poof. Like a magician mid-trick.

Now, a reasonable person might've accepted fate and moved on.

But I'm not that person.

I had put in too much effort. Too many polite reminders. So, I did what I do best: followed up. Gently at first. Then not so gently. A few well-crafted messages later (which in hindsight may have sounded mildly desperate), the vet responded.

He couldn't see Apollo himself, but he offered a backup plan. His junior would examine him, and he'd consult over the phone. Not ideal, but at that point I'd take anything short of a vet appointment via Zoom.

We went in, explained everything to the junior, probably more than he needed to know. He took notes, called the boss, and after some back and forth, we had a diagnosis plan: bring Apollo back the next morning on an empty stomach. No food and no water for twelve hours.

That's when I stopped being a dog mom and became a full-blown Indian mother. Because sure, tests, X-rays, sedation, I understood all of that. But denying him food? My heart cracked a little right there in the clinic.

The vet was still talking, something about medical accuracy and safety, but all I could hear was: "You will starve your son."

And listen, Apollo isn't just any dog. He's a fluffy, four-legged emotional sponge. He eats with joy, like it's his job. He follows me to the kitchen like a food inspector. How was I supposed to look into those big, trusting eyes and say, "No food today, baby?"

So, I hatched a plan. A full-blown containment strategy. He'd be in the air-conditioned room. No distractions. No mention of food. Toys placed exactly where he liked them.

In the middle of all this planning, I started feeling worse. I'd been nursing a cold, but standing in that vet clinic with dander floating around like fairy dust and a dozen animals exhaling near me, it escalated. My nose had become a faucet, and I looked like one of those emotional pet parents who cry at the vet's office.

To everyone there, I was "that lady" clutching her dog like he was heading into surgery, quietly sobbing in the corner. But in reality, I was just severely allergic to most of the creatures in that building. A truly tragic misunderstanding.

Reflection of the day:

Persistence gets things done, but allergies will always get you first.

7th March 2025

I think I lost my sense of humour somewhere today.

Nothing, and I mean nothing, prepares you for the heartbreak of withholding food and water from your dog. Especially, when your baby looks at you with big, confused golden retriever eyes, wondering why his food giving human mommy has suddenly turned so heartless.

But rules are rules. And, tough love is really a thing.

We took Apollo to the vet's clinic, and everything suddenly felt slower. Time didn't just pass; it dragged its feet. I kept glancing at the clock, then at him, and then back again. The air felt heavier than it should've. Was he okay? When will I able to feed him again? Would he forgive me? Would I forgive myself?

And then just like that, the vet sedated him. Apollo went from being an anxious puppy to a floppy, snoring teddy bear in two seconds flat. And, of course, instead of worrying, I found myself cooing, "*Aww, look at him, he's so cute when he's knocked out!*" The irony of this moment was not lost on me.

Now for some context: I was never a dog person. I didn't imagine myself as someone who'd spend her weekend obsessing over a dog's hydration levels. But here I was, hovering over Apollo like a helicopter parent, asking follow-up questions and waiting for test results like it was a medical entrance exam.

The vet shared his medical wisdom, and eventually, Apollo was hooked up to an IV to rehydrate.

We brought him back home, and the next phase began. Watching. Waiting. My brain had already jumped ahead to the next milestone: feeding him.

And let me tell you, nothing, truly nothing, beats the joy of feeding your dog after a day like this. Watching him eat, watching that little tail wag just once, it was like scoring a hundred on a test. Pure relief. Indian moms are built for this. Human baby or dog baby, we don't rest until we see food disappearing into someone's face.

Today was his day, and everyone knew it. The kids pampered him. He got extra cuddles. Because truth be told he's my favourite child. He doesn't backtalk, doesn't demand new shoes every month, and when he's in trouble, he comes back for a cuddle without holding a grudge. Try getting that from a human child. I dare you.

Now, let's talk about his crimes. He has this talent for stealing from our bedside tables. Pens, remotes, earphones. If it fits in his mouth, it's his. But his real obsession is hand cream. Between my bedside and Aliza's, we've lost at least twelve tubes.

Today, though, he was slower. He moved less, ate less. But he still wagged his tail, still looked at us like we were the best thing that had ever happened to him.

Honestly, that was enough for me.

Reflection of the day:

There's nothing more loyal than a dog or more humbling than being loved by one, even on your worst day.

8th March 2025

Now I've said this before, and I'll say it again, Aliza's concept of time belongs to an alternate universe where clocks are decorative items, not functional devices. Today was just further proof that my child and I are operating in two completely different time zones.

She had an extra math class at school this morning because the school suddenly realised they hadn't wrapped up the syllabus and the exam is, oh, just ten days away. The class was scheduled from 9 to 11 a.m. Very reasonable. Except we left home at 9 a.m.

Let's do some actual math (since we're so hell-bent on catching up with it). The school's 15 minutes away, give or take. Add a few minutes to walk in, climb stairs, take a detour to the washroom, giggle with a friend, etc. So yes, we were going to be late. Was I panicking? No. The version of me who was always on edge, so high-strung and correcting everything and everyone, is now retired. I used to move around the house like a hall monitor, keeping a time check on everyone, pointing out shoes that weren't in their place, and putting away cups lying on the table that should have been in the sink. It was exhausting, mostly for me. I'm learning to let it be and accept that my house and the people in it may not be perfect, but neither am I. I'm choosing not to hover or fix, and it feels lighter this way.

Anyway, the reason for our tardiness? The groundbreaking revelation that she got ready late. Shocker. And yet, the moment we got in the car, I became the villain. Aliza, in all seriousness, expected me to transform into a Fast & Furious stunt driver and make a 15-minute journey disappear in five. She was throwing mini tantrums in the passenger seat, convinced that her lateness was somehow my personal failing.

From the way she was looking at me, you'd think I was hiding a pair of helicopter blades under the car roof. I swear she believed that with just a bit more maternal love and determination, I could switch to "Jet Mode" and land her directly into her classroom via the school's secret helipad for the chronically late.

When I told her very politely that no such feature existed, she looked at me like I'd betrayed her trust. Did that stop her? No. She then suggested that I drive through traffic like a maniac, honk and bulldoze if needed just so she could reach on time. Of course. Let me just commit a few minor traffic violations and possibly a homicide or two so you, my sweet child, can attend math class in peace.

Naturally, I came home and unloaded this madness to Jeh, hoping for some sympathy. Instead, he frowned. I was, apparently, "badmouthing" our daughter. Badmouthing? This child wanted me to reenact Fast & Furious. But sure, let's focus on my tone.

He said it "upset him" when I complained about her. What else would I expect from this man who melts the moment Aliza even looks in his direction. Honestly, she could rob a bank and he'd probably hold the door open. So now I'm sitting here wondering, if I can't vent to him, who do I talk to? Am I just supposed to swallow all this daily madness in the name of being a peaceful, evolved, non-toxic mom?

Anyway, I let it go. Mostly because I had a wedding function to attend. My friends and I did what we do best, we dissected the bride's lehenga, her jewellery, the décor, and of course, the food. We were in top form, playing our roles as fully certified society aunties, and loving every minute of it.

Reflection of the day:

If patience burnt calories, I'd be invisible by now.

9th March 2025

Another Sunday, and yet again, India's playing cricket. I don't know who decided that every weekend needs to be about this, but if someone out there is in charge of planning these never-ending matches, I'd really appreciate it if they took a weekend off.

The morning began with an attempt to be productive. Aliza has her drama exam coming up, so we tried prepping. I say "we" loosely. She believes preparation is for the unimaginative. She's convinced she'll just go with the flow and it'll all work out. Meanwhile, I was sitting there feeling like one of those parents who end up more anxious than the kid, wondering why I was more invested in her lines than she was.

Rumi had a pile of worksheets to finish, which is funny because she hasn't yet accepted the concept of homework. She looked at me and asked, "*Why do I have to do more work at home when I already did work at school?*" Honestly, I didn't have a great answer. She kind of had a point. And if schools shared that point of view, I'd have fewer battles to fight. But no such luck. So, there I was, pretending to be some motivated home tutor, and she was glaring at me like I'd ruined her weekend. Which, to be fair, I probably had.

Then came Apollo's grooming appointment. You'd think it was a quick summer trim. But no, what came back looked like a different dog altogether. He left looking like a golden prince and what returned was... well, his undernourished cousin. Even Apollo wasn't sure what had happened. The girls were horrified. "*He was so fluffy and cute!*" they said, like I'd personally shaved his charm off. I, on the other hand, was celebrating how much less hair would be flying around the house.

By afternoon, screen time rules had collapsed. It was the weekend, and according to the children, that means total amnesty from rules and routine. Exams are next week, but that was just a minor inconvenience. And then, of course, all eyes turned to the TV for the India match.

Now, ideally, we should have gone to the club with friends to watch it. Kids would've had fun, adults could have socialised, maybe had a drink. But Jeh and I were both feeling too lazy to change out of our pyjamas. The thought of actual pants felt aggressive.

Naturally, denying the children a night out meant we had to compromise somewhere. "*At least let us have chips and snacks!*" they said, as if it were a basic human right. I agreed. I mean, I was already the bad guy for not taking them out, why make it worse? They tore through the pantry and came out clutching every snack I had mentally budgeted for the next two weeks. It lasted about 45 minutes.

And yes, India won. There was cheering, shouting, general excitement and for a short while, everyone was in a good mood.

But me? Not so much.

Here's the thing. My ideal Sunday would be simple: wake up late, take a long, quiet shower without anyone knocking on the door, go out for lunch, maybe catch a movie with Jeh, and meet a friend for coffee in the evening. Something small but just mine. But these days, Sundays aren't mine.

And to top it off, Aliza has her drama class every Sunday. The driver's off on Sundays, which means I'm the one who takes her. I actually don't mind. It gives me an excuse to leave the house. Driving alone, even for ten minutes, sometimes feels like a mini holiday.

But today, Jeh casually said, "*Why don't you check if her friend's mom could pick her up?*" and I snapped inside. Just like that. It wasn't even what he said, it was how it made me feel. Like I had to justify stepping out. Like I wasn't allowed to want a little space. I don't even think he realised how that comment affected me, but it did. It felt controlling and suffocating. And it made me angry.

Sometimes I really wonder how different things would be if I weren't married. Not in some big way. Just... would I still have to explain myself for small things?

Would I get to make choices without a subtle undercurrent of someone else's opinion?

So yeah, I was mad at him today. He didn't even notice. He just went about his day like everything was fine while I carried the weight of yet another invisible argument in my head.

Reflection of the day:

Sometimes the match isn't on TV. It's the one playing silently in your own head and you're the only one who knows the score.

10th March 2025

Monday mornings always start the same way, with me making up for all the exercise, I conveniently take a holiday from over the weekend. And by weekend, I mean my personal weekend, which starts on Friday... sometimes Thursday. So, to compensate, I heroically extended my usual one-hour workout to a slightly longer one hour and five minutes. Balanced life.

Holi is just around the corner, and since I've accepted my fate as the official HR manager of this project, my visit to the farm was mainly to figure out when the workers will conveniently disappear for their holidays.

While at the farm, I spotted a bunch of raw bananas, and like a true Indian mom, my brain immediately screamed "banana chips!" Healthy, homemade, and, most importantly, approved by my children, which is rare because most of my well-intentioned "healthy snacks" are met with disgust and betrayal. But banana chips? Those make the cut. And since they're made from a fruit, technically, I can tell myself that I'm feeding my children fruit.

Then back to the office site, where work was moving at its usual snail pace.

Later in the evening, when I put on Netflix, Meghan Markle's new show caught my attention. I decided to watch it because, well, who doesn't love a little cringe entertainment?

Within the first three minutes, Meghan was proudly telling the world that she likes to make guests feel at home. How, you ask? By preparing bath salts for them and repacking pretzels in a bag with a handwritten label. The emotional labour of it all! That's it. That's where I turned off the show.

But those three minutes left me inspired. My sister-in-law was arriving from the US at midnight, and suddenly, my *desi* hospitality kicked in. Meghan Markle had bath salts and labelled pretzels? Big deal. I went full-on Pinterest Mom mode.

I took two mason jars, labelled them neatly, and filled them with homemade banana chips and cookies. The kids had been asking for those cookies for days, so I felt like I was finally delivering on a long-pending promise. Then, riding on this strange wave of confidence, I shifted into full host mode.

I put fresh flowers in the room because waking up to something pretty just feels good. I got the kids to write little welcome notes. Meghan had her labelled pretzels and curated goodies, while I had handwritten letters in sketch pen that felt far more honest. Since I was already feeling unusually organised, I added a set of fancy organic body wash and lotion from the stash I keep hidden for "special gifting moments."

The banana chips were from the farm, the cookies were freshly made, the flowers were smelling nice and the whole setup looked like I had spent days planning it. No one needed to know that I threw it all together after finishing a Netflix show and feeling unusually capable for twenty minutes.

By the end of it, I'd officially outdone Meghan Markle. She married a prince; I married Jeh, who, for the record, thinks handing me a cup of tea without being asked is peak romance.

Reflection of the day:

Netflix, if you're listening, I'm ready for my own series. Title suggestion: *Desi* Hosting, No Crown Required!

11th March 2025

Woke up late today, not in a way where you feel all cozy and rested. Nope. The crap-crap-crap we overslept the kids missed school kind of way.

Not that it mattered much because neither of them had plans to go anyway. Aliza had her drama exam in the afternoon, and Rumi had priorities. Her *bua* had flown in from the US last night, and she wasn't about to miss out on prime gifting time.

Now, don't get me wrong, she loves her *Bua*. She really does. But she also loves the list of things she had casually sent her a month ago. To be fair, she did make a decent attempt at masking her intentions, saying she wanted to "spend time" with her *Bua*. And she did. Right after she conducted a thorough inventory check of her new loot.

I've noticed something about Rumi. She loves family. It's not just about the presents (okay, mostly not). She has this constant longing for everyone to be together. She's the type of child who will spend all day in the room of whichever out-of-town relative is visiting, just to soak in their presence. She's the one who asks why *Nana* and *Nani* live so far away, and why *Bua* doesn't stay in India. Aliza was never like this. She was quite happy being the queen of her castle, ruling her own space. Rumi, on the other hand, wants a full house. The more the merrier. If she had it her way, we'd have relatives in every room and a family group hug every evening.

Anyway, the *Bua* who Spoils Nieces lived up to her title. The kids were overjoyed. Even I was overjoyed because my Meghan Markle level hospitality got an official stamp of approval.

Now, back to Aliza. The drama exam was scheduled for 2 pm. At least, that's what I was told. I spent the entire morning mentally preparing myself to handle the high-stakes pre-exam stress.

But Aliza was operating on her own timeline. She casually picked out her dress barely an hour before we were supposed to leave, then took her sweet time drying her hair like she was getting ready for a brunch, not a drama exam. Then she spent an excruciating amount of time on shoes. Every pair I suggested was met with a dramatic eye roll. Especially the ones I had actually spent time and money picking out for her, those were immediately tossed aside. She wanted something "cool but not too much," "grown-up but still age appropriate," and of course nothing in the house matched her vibe. But we didn't have time or options, so she grudgingly settled for the least offensive while I was in the background having what felt like a mild cardiac episode, silently calculating how late we were going to be.

Despite all odds, we made it sharp at 2 pm. And it turned out her teacher had changed her slot to 3 pm.

It was an afternoon in March. The heat was sitting heavy in the air, and the only available seating option was a wooden bench outside with a leafless tree as the shade. Simply fantastic.

After roasting for a few minutes, I called a friend who lived nearby and escaped to her house for some much-needed air conditioning, and some coffee.

Five minutes later.

Aliza called.

"Mom, I feel weird without you here. Can you come back?"

Wait, what? My teenager, who pretends I don't exist in public, suddenly wanted me back? This was huge.

Heart melting, I rushed back, prepared to bask in this unexpected moment of mother daughter love. And the second I got there, she went back to pretending I didn't exist.

But I knew the truth. She needed me there. Just within five feet of her. That was enough.

Today, I discovered something precious. My not so little girl still needs me around. Maybe not openly, but in the quiet, unspoken way that really matters.

And that made today the best day ever.

Reflection of the Day:

Sometimes, all our kids need is to know we're there. Not in their face, not hovering, just there. At a five feet distance, preferably.

12th March 2025

We were up at the crack of dawn, dressed and caffeinated, as we had a meeting with the school principal for Aliza's subject selection. Apparently, ninth grade is the new twelfth grade, and your future hinges on whether you love Chemistry or think Economics sounds mid.

The principal had summoned us for a wholesome little chat about Aliza's strengths and interests. But nobody warns that talking about your child in front of their school authorities is treated like you have just opened their private diary and read it out loud.

I don't know what secret code exists between teenagers and their sense of privacy, but everything seems to be classified. Even saying, "*She likes reading fiction*" is treated like you have let out her big secret. The meeting itself was simple. The principal asked what Aliza enjoys, what she doesn't, and what we see her leaning toward. We answered. Thoughtfully, I might add.

We told her she's good at creative stuff, hates Math, finds French interesting and lights up when she has a story to write. But the look Aliza gave us was something like that scene in Matilda where she glares at the TV and it explodes. Same energy. And I was the TV.

She huffed and puffed all the way back home. According to her, I was talking like a total weirdo and Jeh was not helping either. Basically, we were both out of touch and should have just sat there smiling like statues.

She didn't say it in so many words, of course. She just let her icy silence do the talking, along with those laser beam eyes that said, *"I will never forgive you for saying I used to love painting."* I offered her a snack from my bag as a peace offering, only to get the same death stare in return.

We came home, hoping to decompress and nurse our parental wounds with tea, but life had other plans. Within minutes, we were swept into a full-blown family "conversation."

My sister-in-law had flown in from the US to surprise my in-laws. It was a lovely gesture, but within a day of her arrival, emotions were already running high. My in-laws, though overjoyed, also told her how much they had missed her and how little they got to see her.

She, still recovering from jet lag, tried to explain that hopping across continents is not exactly like dropping by the corner store for milk. But somehow the tone got lost in translation, and before we knew it, everyone was rehashing who visited whom, how many times, and why this cousin came more often than that one.

I still don't know how Jeh and I got pulled into it. One minute we were quietly watching from the side, just nodding at all the drama like sensible bystanders, and the next we were right in the middle of it. I kept muttering a few safe things like, "*Hmm, yes, true,*" while slowly sliding my chair back, wishing I could melt into the wall.

Then Jeh, in a noble attempt to change the topic, casually asked if we wanted some tea and biscuits, and that somehow triggered a full-blown debate about which bakery makes the best ones and someone saying, "*You never listen to me!*"

By the time it all wrapped up, it was 5 p.m. No decisions were made, but we all agreed to enjoy the refreshments. So, peace was restored the traditional way.

Reflection of the day:

Ninth grade subject choices are easier to figure out than family emotions, but both can cause spontaneous migraines.

13th March 2025

It didn't even occur to me that it was *Choti Holi* until Rumi asked me why people set wood on fire the night before *Holi*. That's when I realised that I had just forgotten the day. So, I decided to do what my grandmother did on this day when I was growing up.

I dusted off old memories and told Rumi the story of *Holika* and *Bhakt Prahlad*. I pulled a half-decent version of the *Holika Dahan* story out of the corners of my brain. How good eventually wins over evil, how the aunt tried to burn the nephew, and how he walked out unscathed while she didn't. She listened quietly, which with Rumi, means she's fascinated.

It was a strange feeling, sharing this story. We've always told our kids that people come before religion. That being kind matters more than belonging. But the thing is, I grew up in a *Hindu* household and I grew up hearing this story every single year. Not just hearing it, feeling it. The warmth of the fire and my grandmother's voice narrating the story. Festivals like *Holi* meant being home and being safe.

And even though I no longer feel like running around with colour all over my face, my kids clearly do. Aliza may have passed this phase, but Rumi wanted to celebrate this occasion like how it is truly meant to be celebrated with colours, balloons and *pichkari*.

This year I was completely unprepared, though. I did not even have a token packet of *gulaal*. For a moment I thought I'd just tell her Holi was cancelled. But guilt and nostalgia took over and made me turn to BlinkIt. I panic-ordered whatever Holi-related thing showed up first. Colours, water balloons, and some very heavy duty *pichkaris*.

I felt like such a responsible parent who had it all figured out. Not because I did something amazing, but because I showed up. Even if that meant swiping through an app. That has to count for something.

And you know what, it did. When Rumi saw the pile of *Holi* stuff, her face lit up in that very specific way kids light up when they realise their parents didn't forget something important to them. She didn't say thank you. Of course not. She just walked off with the stuff and a plan I didn't want to hear about. But that smile was enough.

Later in the evening, when the *Holika* fire started in the neighbourhood, I stood there feeling something I hadn't in a while. That tiny flicker of connection between the life I had and the life I'm building for them. It was warm. And this time, not from the fire.

Reflection of the day:

I forgot *Holi* but remembered to act like I didn't, which is basically parenting in a nutshell.

14th March 2025

Waking up late on a holiday is one of life's greatest pleasures. You stretch, yawn, and bask in the knowledge that there's no rush or alarms blaring in your ear. But before I could fully embrace this lazy morning, reality smacked me in the face in the form of one extremely excited 8-year-old.

Rumi was buzzing with the *Holi* spirit. She had been up, planning, and mentally preparing her troops (which is to say, us) for maximum festive participation.

Meanwhile, Aliza had announced her official retirement from *Holi*.

I was stunned. Just last year, this child was sprinting around, armed with water balloons and colour, determined to leave no one unscathed. And now? She joined my sister-in-law, who left the water and colour play years ago.

This is what happens when a child turns 13, apparently. One minute, they're dousing you in colour, the next, they're too cool for *Holi*, too mature and sophisticated to get their hands dirty.

But Rumi? There was no way she was letting us off easy. And honestly, that's one of the things I adore about her. She's all in when it comes to celebrations. Birthdays, anniversaries, festivals. Whatever the occasion, she's the first to dress up, gather everyone, and make sure it feels special. "Let's just take it easy today" is not in her vocabulary. If there's even the slightest reason to celebrate, she's making sure we do it right.

So even though Jeh and I would have much rather lounged around in peace, we weren't about to kill that enthusiasm. We stepped outside, we played, we got drenched in colour, and we had the absolute best time.

Though the house told another story. My bathroom floor was covered in streaks of colour, Apollo had taken on a pink tint that he seemed quite unaware of, and the colour had found its way into places I truly didn't think it could reach.

And the day wasn't over yet.

Jeh and I had a *Holi* party to attend. And being the mature, responsible adult that I like to think I am, I did something truly brilliant. I dressed up for an event that clearly said "no colour."

I even pulled out my old white *kurta*, the dependable one, because why not lean into the theme if the host claims there will be no colour. I trusted the invite. That was my first mistake.

We walked in and immediately realised the invitation had been interpreted very freely. People were already covered head to toe. "No colour" seemed to mean "Do whatever you want, just don't blame us later." Before I could gather my thoughts, a few enthusiastic guests had already smeared colour on my face, and my pure white *kurta* was well on its way to becoming modern art.

The party itself was great, but by the time we got home, Jeh and I looked like two tie-dye samples.

Reflection of the day:

This *Holi* has taught me that kids grow, and sometimes the only thing to do is loosen your grip a little.

15th March 2025

I drove down to the office site, half hoping, to see if the missing labourers had finally decided to show up again after disappearing for *Holi* holidays.

What was I even thinking? Of course they hadn't.

I couldn't tell whether I wanted to laugh or sigh at my own optimism.

The supervisor stood there, without an ounce of shame, and goes,

"*Madam, Holi tha na... isliye.*"

That's it. That was the explanation.

As if *Holi* is now a festival followed by two weeks of memory loss.

I nodded politely like a well-raised woman, but in my head, I was mixing cement and grouting him into the nearest wall.

I came home muttering under my breath, fully prepared to ruin everyone else's mood too. But one of my closest friends was at the door. Just like that. Lunch drop-in. Like the universe sent her because it knew I was dangerously close to losing it.

We hadn't met in ten days. That's basically a year in female friendship time.

We didn't waste a second on "so nice to see you" crap. Straight to the point.

Are we perimenopausal or just permanently tired?

Which anti-ageing serum is the latest scam but we'd still buy it anyway.

We ate reheated *bhindi* and stale *dal* but somehow it tasted better than anything I've eaten at a restaurant in months. Honestly, that conversation fixed more things in me than any spa ever has.

Later in the evening, I went to the salon with my sister-in-law. We had a party to attend later at night. Since I had no new clothes and no real will to try, I went for a blow-dry instead. It felt like the easiest way to look presentable without actually making any effort. I thought I'll just let the hair do the work and hoped no one looks too closely at the rest of it.

Came home, feeling vaguely hopeful about the night, only for Jeh to casually announce he's not coming to the party!

"*Just don't feel like it.*" He said.

I didn't even argue or blink.

Because if marriage has taught me anything, it's how to conserve my energy. To pick my battles wisely.

So, I went.

Said hello to people I hadn't seen in months, while we all acted as if we meet every other weekend. Nodded through conversations I could barely hear because of the background music.

When someone asked, "Where's Jeh?" I gave the standard diplomatic reply. Something about work and travel. Just enough to move the conversation along.

I talked about schools, holiday plans, and the weather. All the reliable small-talk topics that fill space without meaning much.

And honestly, I wasn't miserable.

I left the party in exactly 54 minutes as showing up was enough and no one was handing out trophies for staying through dessert.

Came back, wiped off half my makeup as I didn't have too much energy. Got into bed and spent an hour doom scrolling Instagram, watching strangers declutter drawers, and make smoothies I'll never try. I was half dead but somehow felt weirdly alive.

Reflection of the day:

Blow-dry good. Husband useless.

Bhindi surprisingly healing.

16th March 2025

You know how Sundays are supposed to be like... lazy mornings, late breakfasts, kids watching TV, moms sipping on coffee in peace? Ya. Well. Not this Sunday. Sunday before exams equals no Sunday. It is just another weekday in disguise.

The whole morning was full-on revision with worksheets, and me running between rooms because apparently the younger one and the older one can't revise peacefully in the same space. One says, *"She's humming!"* Another says, *"She's writing too loudly!"*

Anyway, after surviving the morning, Jeh and I thought this was enough. Let's just step out for lunch and give everyone a break. I was expecting more arguments and sulking, when we somehow pulled off the impossible. We all agreed on the same coffee shop. I almost wanted to frame the moment.

With my in-laws' 50th wedding anniversary coming up this Friday, which their adoring children are throwing for them, we had a whole meeting with the decorators in the evening. They wanted old photos for the decor. And obviously, that meant the old albums came out. Actual albums, not phone folders. I swear this part was the nicest bit of the day.

Aliza and Rumi were seeing these black and white childhood pics of their grandparents and their dad for the first time. And Jeh was full-on explaining the stories behind each photo. "*This was the summer we went to Coonoor*" and "*See this one, your Grandpa used to drive this old Ambassador!*"

It was honestly so cute.

And then my sister-in-law also joined in with her own stories, and the girls were so mesmerized. Suddenly history wasn't boring anymore. This sort of history of old pictures and family stories, that I don't mind looking and listening to. Unlike school history, which I always hated. Russian Revolution, *kya karoon main?*

And now that I think about it, Jeh and Rumi have such similar faces in those photos. Same crooked smile, same "caught being naughty" expressions. It was so cute.

Anyway, after all that, we had the big family dinner. We ordered food from various places and ended up with a multi-cuisine spread. I obviously tried everything and thoroughly enjoyed myself. Spent about 10 minutes feeling guilty about overindulging, then finally told myself Sunday is a legit binge day and moved on.

Reflection of the Day:

History class bored me to death, but give me old family albums and I am suddenly taking notes.

17th March 2025

Flew to Delhi today for some retail therapy. It was my sister-in-law's idea and I jumped in. She needed to shop, though of course I knew I'd end up picking up a few things too. How can one not.

But the mom guilt had started building up three days ago. You'd think I was leaving for two weeks, not two days. But no, the mind was already on a loop. Will the kids study? What will they eat?

So, this morning, I turned into some kind of command centre. Printed out revision worksheets for the girls, neatly stapled and labelled. As if they were going to even look at them. But still, it made me feel better to leave a little "study plan."

Then the cook was called. A full two-day menu was written out, breakfast, lunch, dinner, snack options. Healthy and balanced at least on paper. Because given half a chance, they would live on Maggi and Nutella.

I even assigned a few chores to Jeh. The poor thing looked completely trapped. Like he would have much preferred to hop on the flight with me than manage my list.

And because clearly, I don't trust anyone, I even went to the office site. Just to make sure everything was in order. As if the place might spontaneously burn down in the 48 hours that I would be away. But there I was, walking around like some building inspector.

Finally, late in the evening, sitting in the car on the way to the airport, somewhere after the first traffic light, I felt it, that tiny, delicious feeling of freedom. Two days without "*Mummy, where is my...*"

Just me, shopping, and nothing in between.

Reflection of the day:

I basically staged a military operation just to disappear for two days.

18th March 2025

Waking up this morning in my parents' house at this age felt exactly like being twelve again. Except now there are more under-eye circles and an adult's supposed ability to say no to people.

By 8:30 am, I was already halfway through a four-course breakfast. Soaked almonds, *poha, dahi, paratha*, two kinds of *chutneys*, fresh fruit. And still, my grandmother was commenting, as always, on why I was eating so little. I tried to wriggle out of this breakfast marathon, but there was no point. Even before I could finish what was on my plate, more food kept appearing magically.

Somewhere in between all this, my sister, sister-in-law and I were busy planning how we would conquer the Delhi shopping scene in just eight hours.

My sister and I are twins, so we've basically lived one long, shared wardrobe life. Clothes, shoes, bags, everything. Even today, we depend on each other to move things between our two cities because we already know they will fit without a single trial. She is my exact size, my exact height, my exact shoe size. We now treat each other as less of a sibling and more as each other's free personal shopping outlet.

Before our Delhi shopping, she was put in charge of making a list of the best places to shop based on what we needed, and she did.

Right around the time the third course ended and the fourth one landed on the table, we had somehow already sorted everything out. The plan for the day and what we were hoping to find. We even mentioned a budget just to be polite, fully aware that none of us had any intention of sticking to it once we stepped into the first store.

Since this was Delhi and our first stop was a fancy exhibition, we could not simply leave the house. We had to arrive. After some outfit changes, and selecting the perfect handbag, we finally left the house looking, as my father observed, ready for a photo shoot.

We reached the exhibition and wandered from stall to stall. Admiring, trying, bargaining and convincing ourselves that everything was an investment piece.

We bonded over which lehenga colours made us glow and debated at length whether pointy heels were still in fashion.

Our final stop was good old South Ex, my happy place. The nostalgia of growing up in Delhi washed over me. We ended up in one shop for three entire hours. And of course, since we were in South Ex, I had to introduce my sister-in-law to the legendary South Ex *bhel puri*. The one I had loved eating while growing up. That one bite brought back so many happy memories.

But the food coma was far from over because my mother had decided to make *chaat* for dinner. The entire family gathered around to eat *golgappa*, *dahi bhalla*, *papdi chaat* and the works. While eating, we gave everyone a detailed recap of what we had bought, and what we absolutely had to go back for the next day.

My father, eager to be part of the conversation, began suggesting which markets we should visit next. We all nodded politely, knowing very well that the plan was already decided. But his enthusiasm was touching.

Reflection of the day:

When in Delhi, calories and budgets are nothing but vague ideas you only pretend to care about.

19th March 2025

Our return flight was at night. Which, in theory, meant half a day to shop. The plan was simple. Wake up, breakfast, dash out, do damage in the markets, race home, pack everything, and head to the airport.

Except, that is not how life unfolds when you are surrounded by women of the family.

My mom, my sister, my sister-in-law and I were sitting at the table for breakfast when someone innocently mentioned family dynamics . Before we knew it, one story led to another. Soon advice was being handed out generously. Emotional knots were being untangled. It had turned into an impromptu therapy session and everyone was happily participating.

Somehow, without us noticing, the morning had already turned into noon. So much for our power shopping morning. We rushed to get ready and since breakfast had turned into brunch, my mother decided that her elaborate *dal baati choorma* lunch would now be served as an early dinner.

So, we headed out, determined to squeeze in a last round of shopping. There was a certain madness to it, running in and out of stores with the clock ticking in our heads. It may have burnt a few calories, though our big breakfast probably cancelled that out.

We got home and frantically started packing. The suitcases somehow looked smaller than they had in the morning. Anyone who has tried to pack after an enthusiastic shopping spree knows that this is not a task for the weak. Clothes and bags were spilling out in every direction. We sat on our suitcases, arranged, rearranged, and tried every possible trick, but the math wasn't working.

Thankfully, my parents were landing in my city in two days for my in-laws' 50th anniversary, so we did the smart thing and handed over a chunk of our shopping for them to bring along.

And the funny thing is, I didn't even feel that usual end-of-trip heaviness. Knowing I'd see them again so soon made the whole goodbye feel more like, "Okay, see you in 48 hours," rather than a sentimental farewell.

We sat down for the much-awaited *dal-baati-choorma dinner*. It was as good as ever, and we all ate with utmost satisfaction.

Soon it was time to leave. We loaded our suitcases into the car, said quick goodbyes and settled in. Just as we were about to drive away, my grandparents came outside to wave us off. That moment tugged at my heart. While I would see my parents again in two days, I did not know when I would next visit my grandparents. That quiet little goodbye stayed with me all the way to the airport.

Reflection of the day:

No matter how perfectly you plan a day, the heart always finds its own way to remind you what matters most.

20th March 2025

One day to go. Tomorrow is my in-law's 50th wedding anniversary party. 70 people at home. 70!! Jeh, me and my sister-in-law were excited for sure , but also felt the pressure of hosting in the best way possible.

Now technically, everything is outsourced. Décor, catering, DJ. So, on paper, it all looked very easy. But anyone who's hosted a party at home knows there is a whole lot of invisible work involved. The stuff that doesn't show on Instagram, but can make or break your party.

Someone had to track how many extension cords were there in the house and figure out where the damn tissue boxes were kept.

At some point, the women of the family including Aliza did outfit trials to finalize who would be wearing what. Serious decisions were taken about which jewellery matched our outfits the best.

There were also last-minute panic calls to take hair appointments and order toilet paper. Why is it always the toilet paper?

Of course, my husband made the speaker system his personal project of the year. Testing one-two-three and all, basically, anything except doing any actual prep.

Finally, we all sat in the living room with cups of chai and coffee, staring at the to-do lists. The party may be tomorrow, but, the actual success of the party depended on today. The madness and the stress. Because if everything went well today, then tomorrow we would just pour wine and pretend this entire thing came together miraculously.

Reflection of the day:

Hosting a big party is like wearing Spanx, the effort stays hidden but is absolutely necessary.

21st March 2025

The day started early, with my parents landing in the morning and some close family flying in from Bombay. The moment they walked in, the entire house woke up. The kids were thrilled, partly because the house felt full again, and partly because they knew no one was policing their screen time.

Lunch got shifted upstairs to our floor because the decorators had completely taken over downstairs. Lights, flowers, candle stands, men standing around holding ladders and arguing about what should go where. It was a scene. So, we chose the lesser mess upstairs.

Soon enough, the thing we were all secretly hoping for made its entrance. The chocolate meringue. Our Bombay aunt arrived with her ingredients, walked into the kitchen like it was her stage, and got straight to work. She has been making this dessert for years, and Jeh's entire family has a deep emotional attachment to it. It is not just any dessert. It is a tradition.

Rumi was glued to her side, acting like her tiny sous-chef, helping her decorate it. Once ready, the meringue was placed on the counter and within minutes, it was gone. I am not exaggerating. Some of us skipped actual lunch just to make space for it.

After that, the hours blurred. Between greeting people, checking on the setup, running to the salon, and getting dressed, I don't even remember looking at the clock.

We had asked the photographer to come thirty minutes early for family pictures. Of course, someone was still doing their eyeliner, and someone else was still hunting for the right pair of shoes. In the end, we got around ten minutes where the whole clan looked decent enough to photograph.

The pictures were a mix of half-posed, confused expressions which, with a little help from correct editing, will become "candid" once framed.

The evening itself was lovely. The house looked beautiful, the food was genuinely good, and everyone had made an effort. A few of my in-laws' close friends spoke. Sweet and heartfelt.

Then it was Aliza's turn. She had written a small speech for her grandparents, and she read it out with so much calm and sincerity that the room actually went quiet. For a few seconds, everyone looked at her like she had achieved something extraordinary. And honestly, she had. The number of people who came up to me after, saying how mature and thoughtful she is, how composed she seems for her age, left me glowing. I nodded politely, pretending to be the "always composed" mother, while feeling like a balloon filled with pride.

The night ended late. Jeh, my sister-in-law and I had pulled every string to make this evening work. Watching it all fall into place, seeing everyone smiling, laughing, eating, chatting, felt incredibly rewarding.

Reflection of the day:

My earrings were heavy, but nothing weighed more than the mom pride I carried tonight.

22nd March 2025

The day after the anniversary should have been reserved for lying horizontal in pyjamas and not speaking unless absolutely necessary. But of course, that didn't happen.

Because my mother-in-law had other plans. Quite generous plans. And we weren't complaining. She wanted to give my sister-in-law and me some jewellery to mark her milestone wedding anniversary. A lovely gesture. So, off we went, the three of us, for what was meant to be a quick trip to the jeweller. But, when three women are involved, there is no such thing as quick.

We sipped tea and went through tray after tray of jewellery. We had long debates about whether we were earring or bracelet people. And we may or may not have spent ten minutes choosing between two pairs of studs that looked very similar.

My sister-in-law was flying back to the US the next day, and it suddenly struck us that she hadn't seen the farm yet. Because obviously, in the days leading up to the anniversary, life had been hectic.

So, after the jewellery pitstop, Jeh picked us up and drove us to the farm. It is still a work in progress. Cement floors, half-done wall paint, and all that. But she genuinely loved it. This was her first time seeing it in its raw state, and the fact that she appreciated the space and could actually visualise the finished version felt like quiet validation. Maybe Jeh and I were not just grown-ups trying to build something. Maybe we were actually doing it and doing it well.

Meanwhile, back home, something wonderful had happened. My kids' exams finally ended. There would be no more early morning revision and no more guilt-tripping them into studying while I secretly scrolled through Instagram in the next room. Everyone could breathe again. Especially me.

A few weeks ago, Jeh had mentioned a work trip to London from the 24th to 28th of March, and the timing couldn't have been more perfect. The kids had a week off. We could drop them off to Delhi with their *Nana-Nani*. No school and no homework. Just London with its cold weather and city walks. The idea of room service and not hearing "*Mummyyyyy*" every ten minutes already felt like a reward.

Reflection of the day:

When God gives, He sends it gift-wrapped. Mine came with jewellery and a child-free flight.

23rd March 2025

Today wasn't as great and felt a bit off. Not in a downbeat disastrous way, just in that slightly empty, awkward way when someone you actually like is leaving.

My sister-in-law was flying back to the US tonight after spending two solid weeks with us. Having someone around who's close to your age, who gets it without you having to explain it, is honestly better than therapy.

She has a teenage daughter who's a few years older than Aliza, so every sarcastic "whatever", and every door slam from my child was met with zero judgement and maximum solidarity. We didn't have to communicate much, just one look across the table and she would understand what I was trying to say.

Because it was her last day, it somehow turned into a family day. Lunch and dinner together was practically a reunion by our usual standards.

Rumi very sweetly made a card and drew a lopsided heart. Aliza scribbled a message in there as if she was forced into doing it.

Jeh, who was clearly a little low about his sister leaving, chose to deal with it in the way most men do. By making jokes all through dinner. He made jokes about airline food and immigration lines.

I didn't say much, just felt a strange sadness that something nice was ending and I was going to miss it.

Reflection of the day:

The house feels quieter. Which should be nice. But it isn't.

24th March 2025

Flew to Delhi this morning to offload the children.

The plan was simple: drop the kids at their *Nana-Nani's* house, escape to London, and pretend for a few days that we were childless millennials with decent sleep cycles and fully functional spines.

My parents were positively giddy. Not because they missed their grandchildren. No, no. That's far too sentimental. They were thrilled because they were getting the grandchildren without their helicopter mother (me), hovering around with her Google-backed theories on screen time and gut health.

So, this time, they made only one request, some might call it a condition: One. Simple. Thing.

"Do not call us. At all. Just go. Live your life. Let us live ours with Ice Cream and Lip Gloss."

Honestly, they weren't wrong. It was strangely liberating to relinquish control and trust that the grandparents would manage. Sure, I knew it would be hectic. The children would likely become semi-feral. The word 'time' in bedtime will cease to exist. Breakfast might be replaced with donuts. And the only physical activity they'd get would be racing through Sephora buying lip-gloss funded by a wildly enthusiastic *Nanu* with zero resistance.

But still. Ignorance is bliss. If I didn't know what was happening, I couldn't interfere. And if I didn't interfere, I could maybe, just maybe actually enjoy myself in London.

So, in the evening, Jeh and I packed up our bags and headed to the airport, feeling oddly care-free. Now here's the funny thing. We suddenly didn't know what to do with ourselves. There was no one asking for Happy Meals. I wasn't lugging around three kinds of hand sanitiser or six emergency snacks. In fact, I didn't even have cabin luggage. I felt like I had lost a limb but gained a life.

Jeh and I looked at each other like two awkward teenagers who'd lied to their parents and somehow gotten away with it. We were giddy with excitement.

Once we got on the flight, we didn't even pretend to be adults anymore and went straight for the TV. He watched a war movie. I watched a romcom. We had entered our own little Netflix nirvana.

For seven hours, we didn't speak or think about our children. We just basked in the rarest form of freedom.

Reflection of the day:

Sometimes good parenting means knowing when to get out of the way and let the grandparents spoil the kids.

25th March 2025

We landed in Heathrow early in the morning and I got that typical feeling of being abroad the moment I stepped out of the aircraft. The air smelt clean and colder. Everyone around was dressed in winter coats and boots while I was such an idiot I thought adding a scarf would keep me warm. My nose had turned red, and my fingers froze but I still felt vaguely excited.

We got to the hotel, which was in South Kensington. Sounds fancy, because it is. It is one of those neighbourhoods where everyone drinks oat milk and takes their dogs out on walks in designer jackets. There are cafes in every corner, the constant background aroma of freshly ground coffee and a tube station next door.

We unpacked, took a power nap, and then stepped out for lunch. The original idea was to eat somewhere close by, but the food scene in this area is genuinely absurd. You name a cuisine, and it exists within a three-minute walking radius. Thai, Japanese, Arabic, French, Ethiopian, Korean, Turkish. It felt like we were standing at the centre of the world with a menu that stretched across continents.

This is the thing about cities like London. They draw people from everywhere, and when people come, they bring their food, their flavours, their memories of home, their entire cultural identity packed into a recipe. You can taste someone's grandmother's Sunday lunch from a country you may never visit. That is what makes big cities feel alive. They give you the illusion that the whole world is within reach.

We spotted a Georgian café serving vegan cheese on sourdough as if it were the most every day, unremarkable thing. In the city I live in, that would be a headline. Here, it was just Tuesday.

We walked up and down the block, quietly debating what we were "in the mood for," but really were just overwhelmed by the choices. Finally, after a little too much indecision, we settled on a Lebanese place. As expected, the food didn't disappoint. And just like that, the city welcomed us.

Post-lunch, in a noble effort to feel cultural, we headed to the Tower of London. I've been before, but it's still fun to wander around pretending to soak up medieval history while actually just scouting for the nearest good coffee.

We ended the day at a pub that looked like it had been there forever and didn't update anything because it didn't need to. The wooden floors were slightly uneven from years of footsteps, and there was a long bar polished not by cleaning but by hands and elbows leaning into it. Yellowed photographs hung on the walls that no one really looked at, but if they were taken down, the room would feel incomplete. There was a quiet hum of voices, not loud, just a steady murmur that sounded like breathing.

The lights were low and soft, and in that light my face looked gentler. The lines around my eyes didn't announce themselves.

The first sip of my drink didn't do anything significant. My shoulders simply dropped a little, and my jaw loosened. The day released its grip. By the second drink, my thoughts stopped running. The world no longer felt like something to manage.

I think it was the lighting that took the years off, and eventually the drinks that convinced me it was true.

Reflection of the day:

Being abroad feels like temporarily borrowing someone else's life.

So far, I'm not in a rush to give it back.

26th March 2025

Jeh had gone off for some essential business work, the whole reason for our trip, leaving the day to myself.

Harrods was a twenty-minute walk from our hotel. A normal person would have called a cab. I decided to walk, just to feel like a local but also to justify the almond croissant I had inhaled like a Dyson vacuum cleaner in the morning. I crossed the Victoria and Albert Museum. Didn't go in, obviously. Just looked at it, felt intelligent for recognising the name, and moved on like the highly cultured woman I pretend to be.

It was so cold, and even though the chilly wind slapped me in the face, it made me feel alive. The wind was playing around with my hair for the better or worse, and the freezing temperature made my eyes all teared-up, but, in all sincerity, all of it all made me feel liberated.

By the time I reached Harrods, my nose had turned red and my fingers had gone numb.

Now, Harrods is not a store. It is a parallel universe where price tags are suggestions and everything, absolutely everything, is scented. I spent the first ten minutes in the handbag section, mentally calculating how many years of school fees I would need to skip to afford a Hermes bag. After that, I got lost somewhere in the home décor section and spent a concerning amount of time staring at a rabbit-shaped candle stand. Why did it cost that much? Why was I seriously considering to buy it?

Eventually, my legs gave up and I found a seat at the Harrods Café. I ordered an almond milk cappuccino just to feel fancy. It tasted terrible. But I sipped on it anyway, mostly for the feeling. Sitting there, surrounded by women with sculpted cheekbones and handbags that could pay rents, I had this odd, peaceful moment where I realised I was exactly where I wanted to be. Alone, and pretending to belong.

I walked back to the hotel, frozen but fully content. Jeh was back, looking pleased with himself as if he had solved world hunger. He asked what I had been up to. I said, "*Just walking around.*" Technically, I wasn't hiding anything, since thankfully better sense had prevailed and I did not buy the three-hundred-and-eighty-pound candle stand.

Later in the evening, we went out for dinner with friends to a cosy Italian place. The food was just fabulous and the wine was flowing as if it were trying to fix your life.

Reflection of the day:

Next time I'm at Harrods, I need to remember to take a selfie outside for Insta.

27th March 2025

Jeh went off to work again but I wasn't complaining. I had plans with an old friend whom I hadn't seen in years.

I managed to board and exit the London tube at the right station despite my anxiety. So, it was definitely a good start to the day. Anyone who doesn't live in London will understand why this tiny victory feels so huge. The tube can be... intense. Everything moves fast. People walk like they're training for the Olympics. The maps have more coloured lines than a child's drawing book. And the doors open and shut with zero interest in whether you made it inside or not.

If you're not used to it, your brain starts doing its own drama. Did I get on the right train? Is this the correct platform? Why are there twelve exits? Where does this staircase go? And why is everyone so calm when I'm sweating through my jacket?

Add to that the pressure of not wanting to look like a confused tourist blocking the doorway, and there you have it. Full-blown tube anxiety.

So, the fact that I managed to get on, stand in the right spot, not panic, not miss my stop, and actually exit at the correct station felt like a small achievement. Honestly, I deserved a medal. Or at the very least, a pastry.

We spent the morning catching up over coffee and stepped out to a park near her place and it looked picture perfect. The air smelt like eucalyptus and I think my lungs sprang a happy dance. There were ponds with fish actually swimming around instead of looking half dead like back home. It all felt so peaceful that it didn't feel like real life. It felt like a sort of place you'd see on a brochure and assume is heavily edited. But no, it was just a regular Thursday in her neighbourhood.

Her little one dashed off after a squirrel, laughing with that pure full-bellied joy you could only expect from little kids. And, I stood there thinking, this is what I want for my girls. The freedom to run wild in nature, without me scanning the area for stray dogs, broken swings, or mysterious smells that usually accompany parks back home. There, I need to carry sanitizer like perfume.

But then, just as I was romanticizing this whole foreign lifestyle, my friend casually mentioned how she hadn't sat down properly since 6 a.m., had reheated her own breakfast thrice and wouldn't get a break until her husband returned at 7. Suddenly, my smelly Indian park and our ever-faithful *helper didi* back home didn't seem so bad.

After wrapping up, we said our goodbyes and I headed off to Covent Garden to meet Jeh. I loved the feel of this place with its cobbled streets, flower carts, musicians around every corner, and beautiful boutiques.

We had a long shopping list. And like most parents, 80 percent of it was stuff for the kids. Socks. Books. Clothes they'll outgrow in three weeks. But we didn't mind. We missed the girls. Even the background noise. Even their whining. Maybe not all the whining but enough of it to not feel guilty while buying that overpriced sweater.

I also bought a bunch of things which I wasn't sure when or how I'll use so I categorised them as "souvenirs."

Reflection of the day:

London parks are beautiful. But so is my house help.

28th March 2025

It was our last day in London. We had an early flight the next morning, so the whole day felt like it was running on a timer. For once, Jeh had no meetings and no calls. It was just the two of us, and the city. We decided to squeeze whatever was left of our holiday and hold it tightly.

We walked to Buckingham Palace and did the usual tourist staring through the iron gates. After that, we wandered to St. James's Park and bought ice cream. I sat down on a bench, ready to enjoy the moment, but didn't.

The last time we sat there, the girls were with us. Rumi had dropped her ice cream within thirty seconds and cried like someone had stolen her childhood. Aliza had sulked because hers didn't come with chocolate chips. I remember wiping sticky hands, hissing threats about cancelling plans, and wondering why we even try to do "fun things" as a family. It was irritating and nowhere close to peaceful.

And now, in that very spot, a quiet ache spread between us. I would give anything to go back to that noisy, ridiculous moment. We didn't say much. We didn't need to. I took out my phone and we scrolled through their old baby photos. Suddenly, the need to gather my little family felt stronger than any travel high.

Later, we walked through Leicester Square and went for a late lunch at Dishoom. I wanted to see what the hype was about, and even though Jeh has a very strict rule against eating Indian food while abroad, he agreed.

We shopped afterwards and bought things we absolutely did not need. Jeh bought an overpriced magnet because it had a red bus and he thought the girls would like it. I picked up a tiny pink coin purse that Rumi would definitely lose within twenty-four hours, but I still bought it because I could already imagine her smile.

Back at the hotel, we opened our suitcases to start packing. I checked the dress I bought for Aliza even though it was already folded perfectly. It made no sense. I checked it again anyway.

We had wanted this break. We had planned it, counted down to it, talked about what we would do first and eat first and buy first. And it was wonderful. It really was. But by the end of the day, we both knew we were ready to go back.

Back to the girls who will drive us mad within the first hour. Back to Rumi fighting over who gets the first hug. Back to Aliza sniffing her dinner and announcing it smells strange. Back to the mess and the noise and the comfort of a home that looks nothing like a postcard but feels exactly right.

Home is where someone is always yelling "*Mummy.*" Home is where nothing is perfect, but everything is ours.

Reflection of the day:

Having children is like watching pieces of your heart wander around the world with their own opinion and moods. And somehow, that turns out to be my greatest adventure of all.

Closing Note

If you've stuck around this far, thank you. For reading, for laughing at the parts that were meant to be funny, and forgiving me for the bits that weren't.

This book began with me wondering if anyone would care about what goes on inside a mother's mind: the running thoughts about what to make for dinner, while also second-guessing whether I've emotionally scarred my children (which is yet to be discussed with a therapist).

I wrote this book to understand myself better. But if any of these pages made you feel seen, or less alone, or even just gave you something to smile about, then that is already more than I ever hoped for.

Now go. Hug your child.

Or ignore them while you finish your tea.

Either way, you're doing great.

And finally, to my parents, grandparents, sister and my husband.

Who I am is because of them.

And who I am, I have grown to love.

So, thank you, truly.

Glossary

Hindi / Phrase	Literal English Translation
Adrak	Ginger
Aloo tikki	Spiced potato patty
Bartan ki dukaan	Utensil shop
Bhabiji	Sister-in-law (respectful term for brother's wife or any married woman)
Bhaiya ji	Elder brother; respectful address to a man
Bhel puri	Savoury snack made of puffed rice, chutneys, and spices
Bhakt Prahlad	Devotee Prahlad – child devotee of Lord Vishnu
Bindi	Decorative forehead dot worn by women
Bua	Father's sister; paternal aunt
Chaat	Savoury street snack with tangy chutneys and spices
Chai	Tea
Choorma	Sweet crushed wheat dish with ghee and sugar

Choti	Braid or plait (of hair)
Choti Holi	"Little Holi"; the day before Holi festival
Chutney	Spicy or tangy condiment made from fruits or herbs
Dal baati choorma	Rajasthani meal: lentils, baked wheat balls, and sweet crushed wheat
Dal chawal	Lentils and rice
Desi	Local; native; traditional (often "Indian")
Dahi	Yogurt
Dahi bhallas	Lentil dumplings soaked in yogurt and topped with chutneys
Dhaba	Roadside eatery serving local Indian food
Didi	Elder sister; also a respectful address for a woman
Dimag ki bimari	"Disease of the brain"; insanity / craziness
Ghee	Clarified butter
Golgappa	Hollow crispy puri filled with flavored water; pani puri
Gulaal	Colored powder used during Holi
Haldi doodh	Turmeric milk
Helper didi	Domestic helper (female); literally "helper sister"
Holika	Demoness burned in Holika Dahan ritual
Holika Dahan	Ritual bonfire symbolising burning of evil

Jyotish	Astrologer
Kya karoon main	"What should I do?"
Kurta	Long loose shirt worn by men or women
Maasi	Mother's sister; maternal aunt
Madam, Holi tha na... isliye.	"Madam, it was Holi... that's why."
Masala	Spice mix
Mummy ke haath ka khana	Food made by mother's hands; home-cooked food
Nana/Nanu	Maternal grandfather
Nani	Maternal grandmother
Pan masala	Flavored areca nut and spice mixture for chewing
Papdis	Crisp fried wafers used in chaat
Paratha	Layered or stuffed Indian flatbread
Parivaar	Family
Pichkari	Water gun for spraying colors (during Holi)
Poha	Flattened rice dish, often spiced
Roti	Indian flatbread made from wheat flour
Vella giri	Idleness; wasting time; doing nothing useful

About the Author

Parul Patel is a full-time mother, part-time wellness enthusiast, and the default go-to person for her husband and kids, for everything from life's big plans to its tiny inconveniences. She documents the mental gymnastics of motherhood with unfiltered honesty and a sharp sense of humor. When she's not solving everyone's problems or negotiating with her children about bedtimes, she's writing about the love and mess that come with raising a family. She lives in India with her husband, two daughters, and a Golden Retriever who she considers as her third child. This is her first book, written in stolen moments between family mayhem and cups of tea that went cold before she could drink them.